The 2

Vittorio Giudici

Illustrations by: Sergio

BARRON'S

DoGi

English translation © Copyright 1999
by Barron's Educational Series, Inc.
Original edition © 1999 by DoGi spa, Florence, Italy
Title of original edition: Il XX secolo: le grandi svolte dell'umanità
Italian edition by: Vittorio Giudici
Illustrations by: Sergio
Editor: Andrea Bachini
Graphic Display: Sebastiano Ranchetti
Art Director: Sebastiano Ranchetti
Page make-up: Sebastiano Ranchetti
Iconographic Researcher: Katherine Carlson Forden

English translation by Anthony Brierley

All inquiries should be addressed to:
Barron's Educational Series, Inc.
250 Wireless Boulevard
Hauppauge, NY 11788
http://www.barronseduc.com

Library of Congress Catalog Card No. 98-76195

International Standard Book No. 0-7641-0944-8

Printed in Italy
9 8 7 6 5 4 3 2 1

Table of Contents

EMPIRES AND REVOLUTIONS: 1900–1914

Scientists were the first innovators of the twentieth century. In the first fifteen years of the nineteenth century the system of European states continued to dominate a world shaken by revolutionary movements and the decline of centuries-old empires.

The century of science

The twentieth century is increasingly often recognized as the century of science. During these decades research and innovation became more and more widespread, thorough, and decisive. In the early years of the century scientists invited people to question the consolidated image that had been established of the universe, matter, and themselves. In the beginning it was a group of mathematicians, physicists, and doctors who looked at the world with new eyes, and it was scientists who recognized the revolutionary nature of the articles published in 1905 by a young German Jew named Albert Einstein. At the beginning of the century the most important breakthroughs were made in the realm of physics. Between 1896 and 1913 the concepts of matter and energy were revolutionized by a series

of new discoveries. The basic unit of all matter, the atom, was no longer seen as a permanent and unchangeable unit, but was recognized as a particle that could be further divided. The French scientists Antoine Becquerel and Pierre and Marie Curie, the British physicists Ernest Rutherford and Joseph John Thomson, and the Danish physicist Niels Bohr, made important discoveries like radioactivity, the complexity of the atom, the means to measure energy and the impossibility of separating energy from matter. In the realm of material invention, the new century got off to a sensational start with the experiments on radio communication that Guglielmo Marconi carried out and the first motorized flight of Orville Wright.

After the telephone
It was the radio that transmitted sounds and the human voice long distances thanks to experiments by various scientists, including Guglielmo Marconi, who in 1901 made the first transatlantic wireless connection, from Cornwall in Great Britain to Newfoundland in Canada.

THE FIRST AIRPLANE
Fueled by gasoline, it was designed by Orville and Wilbur Wright and flew on December 17, 1903 at Kitty Hawk, North Carolina.

Einstein and Freud
Inspired by the new physics of the German scientist Max Planck, Albert Einstein made his own enormous impact on science and culture at the beginning of the century. Unlike many of his colleagues, Einstein did not proceed by experimentation, but through study and reflection. He is therefore considered the founder of theoretical physics. This approach resulted in his special theory of relativity (1905) and his later general theory of relativity (1915). His theoretical premises and the new physics represented a fundamental contribution to many later inventions, including the photoelectric cell, the laser, and the high-tension generator.

Science's new horizons were already extending far out into the immensity of cosmic space, but also deep into the infinitely minute space of subatomic

The Wright airplane
The plane flew about one hundred and thirty feet. Orville Wright turned with the aid of a lateral command.

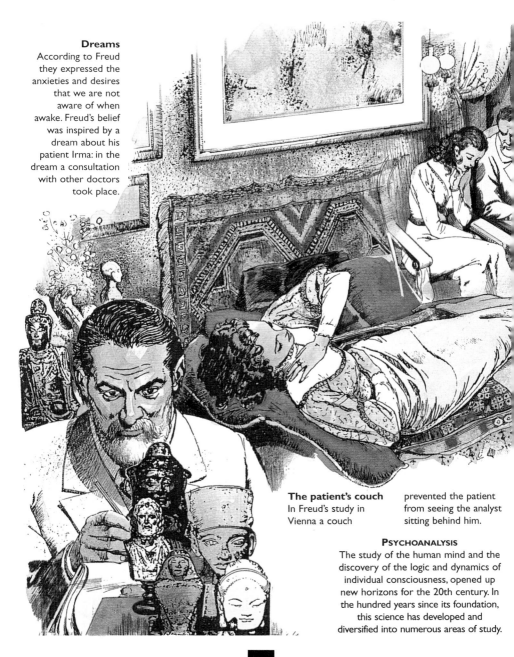

Dreams
According to Freud they expressed the anxieties and desires that we are not aware of when awake. Freud's belief was inspired by a dream about his patient Irma: in the dream a consultation with other doctors took place.

The patient's couch
In Freud's study in Vienna a couch prevented the patient from seeing the analyst sitting behind him.

PSYCHOANALYSIS
The study of the human mind and the discovery of the logic and dynamics of individual consciousness, opened up new horizons for the 20th century. In the hundred years since its foundation, this science has developed and diversified into numerous areas of study.

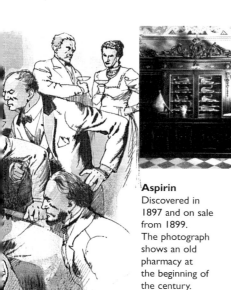

particles. At the same time important new inroads were being made in the study of human identity. A Jewish doctor named Sigmund Freud, a citizen of the Hapsburg Austro-Hungarian Empire, carried out exhaustive studies into the working of the human mind. In doing so, he founded the new discipline of psychoanalysis. On November 4, 1899, bearing the date 1900, *The Interpretation of Dreams* was published. Freud, who was forty-four years old, was convinced that in order to understand the profound nature of human identity, even beyond the traumatic events that filled human lives, it was necessary to search into people's minds and into the unconscious fantasies that appeared in their dreams.

Aspirin
Discovered in 1897 and on sale from 1899. The photograph shows an old pharmacy at the beginning of the century.

Gustav Jung
A Swiss physician who spread psychotherapy but drew away from the ideas of Freud: his analytical psychology was not only a therapeutic technique; it was also a philosophical system.

Marcel Proust
A twentieth century French writer, Proust was one of the principle narrators of the century. His series *A la recherche du temps perdu* offers a portrayal of the changes of three generations.

World population

While scientists were laying the foundations for the future of humanity, population experienced a phase of rapid expansion. From 1850 to 1900 the world population had already increased from 1.2 to 1.6 billion people, with a growth rate of 0.6 percent, higher than any other in history. But these events, although dramatic, cannot compare to what happened in the twentieth century. That in the year 2000 the world's population exceeds 6 billion gives some idea of the population explosion that has taken place.

Demographers who study changes in population figures say that from the seventeenth century a transition occurred. This shift was associated with global agricultural development and its interrelationship with the Industrial Revolution. Death rates fell, while birth rates remained stable. During this period the population of western Europe registered an increase that was proportionately higher than elsewhere. Thus, at the beginning of the twentieth century the life expectancy of a newborn European child was fifty years compared to almost twenty-seven for a newborn Indian. Personal income, improvements in food consumption, and medical services favored the greater longevity of Europeans.

However, the first decade of the twentieth century brought a change in world demographic trends. In Europe the drop in mortality rates was balanced by a decrease in the birth rate. European populations had become increasingly concentrated in cities from the second half of the nineteenth century. Industrialization, education, and changes in lifestyles combined to reduce the number of children. Demographic pressure was further relieved by the exodus of millions of European peasants who emigrated to other parts of the world: Australia, Latin America, the United States, and Canada. In 1910 the growth rate of populations outside Europe rose. This trend became more and more accentuated as the century wore on.

New industries
Transatlantic migrations were carried out on a scale that exceeded any other in recorded history. Those who left the countryside of Europe were favorably received in the United States.

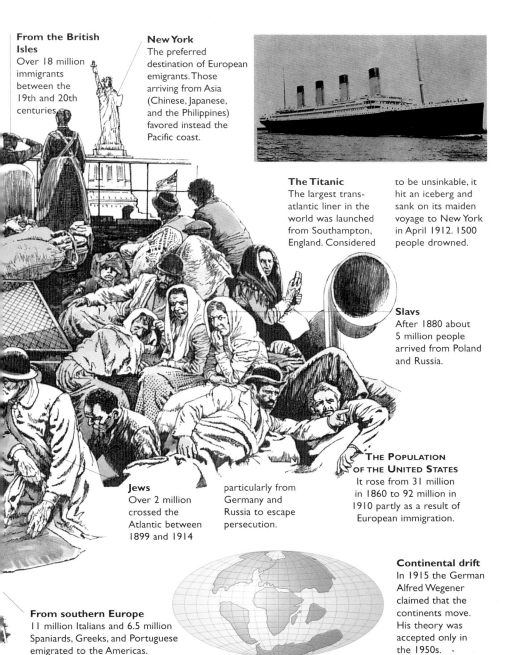

From the British Isles
Over 18 million immigrants between the 19th and 20th centuries.

New York
The preferred destination of European emigrants. Those arriving from Asia (Chinese, Japanese, and the Philippines) favored instead the Pacific coast.

The Titanic
The largest trans-atlantic liner in the world was launched from Southampton, England. Considered to be unsinkable, it hit an iceberg and sank on its maiden voyage to New York in April 1912. 1500 people drowned.

Slavs
After 1880 about 5 million people arrived from Poland and Russia.

Jews
Over 2 million crossed the Atlantic between 1899 and 1914 particularly from Germany and Russia to escape persecution.

THE POPULATION OF THE UNITED STATES
It rose from 31 million in 1860 to 92 million in 1910 partly as a result of European immigration.

From southern Europe
11 million Italians and 6.5 million Spaniards, Greeks, and Portuguese emigrated to the Americas.

Continental drift
In 1915 the German Alfred Wegener claimed that the continents move. His theory was accepted only in the 1950s.

THE ASSEMBLY LINE
This ensured that the various parts of the car arrived at the workers' positions in a particular sequence. Developed in 1913, the assembly line reduced the time it took to build a Ford Model T from 12 hours 8 minutes to 1 hour 33 minutes.

This influx of immigrants had much to do with America's status as a great industrial power and its new leading role on the world scene. Highly mechanized agriculture guaranteed the United States's supremacy in the production of food. During the period of European imperialistic expansion, the United States gave priority to commercial and financial, rather than territorial expansion. In America there was work, and before 1915 the flow of immigrants from Europe reached an average of one million a year. In America even more than in Europe, the development of industry was founded primarily on the concentration of businesses and on the most innovative and rational forms of labor

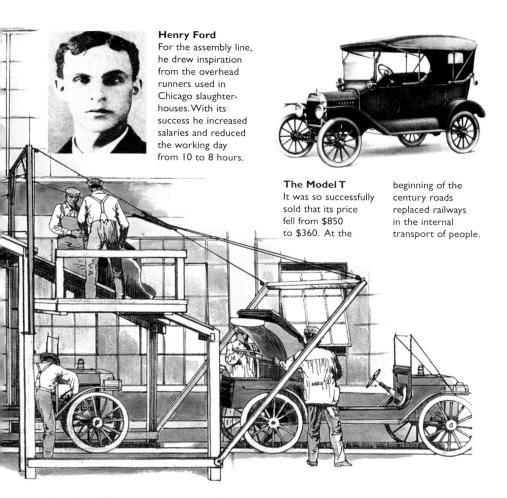

Henry Ford
For the assembly line, he drew inspiration from the overhead runners used in Chicago slaughter-houses. With its success he increased salaries and reduced the working day from 10 to 8 hours.

The Model T
It was so successfully sold that its price fell from $850 to $360. At the beginning of the century roads replaced railways in the internal transport of people.

organization. These were remedies that protected profits and enabled businesses to ride the negative effects of growing competition and price reductions. The assembly line of the Ford factory in Michigan is the best-known example of the application of the new theories of labor organization elaborated by Frederick W. Taylor (1856–1915).

Western society
The increasingly close links between economy and science, and the rapid expansion of the war industry spurred by the growing demand for militarized states, gave rise to a sort of second Industrial Revolution. This development was rooted in the previous century and shaped the new character of Western society.

Political leaders
The growth of the working class created new leaders. Often they were intelligent former factory workers, more confident and educated than workers who came from agriculture.

Workers' parties
Grew rapidly in Europe. They organized and led the working class in their struggle against capitalists and capitalist states. Trade unions fought for better working conditions, 8-hour shifts and higher wages.

Increasingly replaced small workshops with less than ten workers. In the early twentieth century two thirds of the occupants of cities with more than 100,000 inhabitants were in industry.

The widespread spirit of enthusiasm that came after the economic crisis of the late nineteenth century led many to call the years before 1915 the *belle époque*. This term correctly described the increased wealth of the rich, the well-being of the middle classes, the improvement in workers' living standards, and the fall in unemployment. It said nothing however, about the persistence of poverty and social inequalities. A class of employees, technicians, and traders emerged. This, along with the development of the working class and its capacity to organize itself into a political and trade-union movement, brought about the extension of political rights in the West when many countries adopted universal male suffrage, that is, the right of all male adults to vote in political elections.

Women win the right to vote
Women were granted universal suffrage only after World War I. Beginning in the last decade of the eighteenth century in industrialized nations the work of women had assumed increasing importance—Germany, the United Kingdom, France, the United States, and Scandinavian countries. Nevertheless, women slowly acquired political rights due largely to agitation and protests by educated and enlightened representatives of the middle classes. Various factors modified the image and condition of women in the West. They attained increasing levels of education and greater freedom of movement. At the same time, indu-

POLITICAL EQUALITY
POLITICAL EQUALITY
This ideal engaged women in lengthy struggles from the beginning of the century. New Zealand extended the right to vote to women in 1893, Finland in 1906, and Norway in 1913. After World War I it was the turn of Germany, Austria, and the US. In the United Kingdom women were given the vote in 1928, in Spain in 1931, in Turkey in 1934, in France in 1944, in Italy in 1945, in Japan in 1946, in Iran in 1963 and in Portugal only in 1976.

stries and their advertising apparatuses began to pay attention to women's taste and to their recognized influence in deciding family purchases. However, it was the great upheaval generated by World War I, which began in 1914 that marked the cause and beginning of deeper changes and the attainment of universal suffrage.

World politics

Various eminent historians have classified the first fourteen years of the twentieth century as the final phase of a longer period, the so-called Age of Empire, which began in the second half of the nineteenth century.

For a century, from 1815 to 1914, with the exception of various shortlived local conflicts, Europe had experienced no major war. From 1874 onwards no European power had taken up arms against another; instead, each had chosen for its victims the weaker countries of the world outside Europe.

The Europe that dominated the rest of the world, whose most powerful nations possessed a colonial empire, had its own homogeneous identity, an identity usually called Western European civilization. Its main attributes were a capitalist economy, liberal political and judicial systems, the dominance of a large middle class, and a faith and optimism in science and progress. Conscious of their superiority, the European powers—particularly Great Britain—tended to export their economies, that is, the economic and commercial interests of their productive and financial apparatuses, to the rest of the world. Thus, under European dominance, an interdependent world system was created. In the early years of the twentieth century this interdependence began to cause social and political crises and tensions in vast areas of the world that were not subject to European colonial rule, but where

Suffragettes
The two Pankhursts, mother and daughter, were at the head of the movement of English women and were often imprisoned.

THE BOXERS
Members of a xenophobic religious sect which in 1900 attacked railways, missions, and foreign embassies in Beijing (then called Peking).

The "open door" policy
The American approach to penetration in China: equal rights for all countries to carry out commercial activities.

The empress dowager of China
The empress dowager T'zu-hsi, born in 1835, ruled the Chinese empire until her death in 1908. Cruel but intelligent, she steered a middle course between conservatives and reformers.

The coalition
American, British, German, French, Italian, Russian, and Japanese troops reacted to the action of the Boxers and besieged the Forbidden City, the residence of the imperial family.

The Japanese emperor
In 1889 the emperor Mutsuhito granted a constitution that gave civil rights to a minority. At the beginning of the 20th century half of the state budget was used for the army.

conditioned by the interests of Western civilization. It has been said that the latter eroded the foundations of the old social, economic, and political structures of a part of the world that had become peripheral and marginal, a part where until then various centuries-old empires such as China and Persia had flourished.

The nature of world politics in the first fifteen years of the century can be summed up in this way: Europe had lived out its golden *belle époque* and its institutions worked well, despite growing fears about a future war that prompted an increasing recourse to arms. At the margins of Western Europe and the United States, in the vast geographical area of the old empires, as well as other more recent ones, political crises and revolution were the order of the day.

China and Japanese expansionism

The Chinese empire is one of the oldest political institutions ever to have existed. Yet in 1911, after two thousand years of history, it was supplanted by the first Chinese republic. The origins of China's internal crisis dated back to before the arrival of the Europeans, Americans, and Japanese. But the coalition of these foreign powers—expressed in their unified reaction to the Boxer Rebellion of 1900–1901—played a decisive role in the country's destabilization and the dissolution of the empire. The members of the elite class that overthrew the empire attempted without success to modernize the country. In the absence of a strong national regime however, China's weakness continued until the Chinese Communist Party took power in 1949.

At the turn of the century in Japan, following the abolition of feudal serfdom in 1871 and the reform of education, the army and fiscal policy, a new era began. At this time, the army generated an aggressive foreign policy, particularly towards China and Russia; against Russia the Japanese fought and won a war in 1904–1905. Japan was the only one of the old imperial states to have assimilated the lesson of Western Europe: it too had become a modern wolf among wolves.

The empire of the tsar

The peace treaty between Russia and Japan signed at Portsmouth on September 5, 1905 recognized the first astounding victory of a country outside Europe over a great European nation. But Russia was an ailing European empire. Like the Hapsburg Empire during the same period, it was simultaneously backward and advanced. The immense size of its territory and its vast population alone were no longer sufficient to guarantee its rank as a great imperial power. At the turn of the century Russia was forced to come to terms with a number of complex social problems: the long-standing demoralization of millions of peasants, large-scale processes of industrialization resulting in the creation of a strong urban proletariat and the awakening of nationalistic tendencies in such border territories as Poland and the Ukraine.

Strikes
These were rife in Russia at the beginning of the century. Strikers sought higher wages and the reduction of the working day to eight hours.

Battleship Potemkin
One of the most famous films in the history of the cinema, directed by Sergei Eisenstein in 1926 to commemorate the revolution of 1905. It tells of the mutiny in the port of Odessa, which was brutally suppressed by the tsar's soldiers.

St. Petersburg
The 29th of January, 1905, was given the name "Bloody Sunday" because on this day the army fired on a crowd of 140,000 people who had gone to the Winter Palace to present a petition to the tsar.

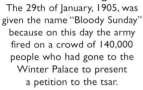

Nevsky Prospekt
In St. Petersburg, in the weeks after Bloody Sunday, for the first time, the working class used the strike as a political weapon.

The unfortunate adventure in foreign policy culminating in the lost war of 1905 sparked the reaction of bourgeois liberals, and revolution broke out in Russia in January 1905. The objective—which was not achieved—was the establishment of a parliamentary democracy and a series of reforms. The result was the continuation of strong social and political tensions up until the outbreak of World War I.

The fall of Persia and Morocco

The imperialistic aims of the major world powers interfered in the internal affairs of another ancient empire, Persia, and of the westernmost of Islamic kingdoms, Morocco. A westernized intellectual class, the powerful merchants of the bazaar, and the Shiite Muslim clergy were the three main components of Persian society, distant from each other but allied against the

THE ISLAMIC WORLD
In 1905 the independent states were the Ottoman Empire, Persia, Saudi Arabia and the other countries of the Arabian peninsula, Morocco and Afghanistan. In all, 41 million Muslims, as opposed to the 160 million in Islamic areas subject to colonial rule.

Morocco
Independent at the beginning of the century, it remained victim of secret agreements between the major powers which in this way controlled one of the few African territories not yet subject to colonial rule.

Persia
Following calls for modernization, a constitution was granted in 1906 but immediately after there were internal conflicts between social and religious forces. Interest in petroleum moved Great Britain towards control of the political situation.

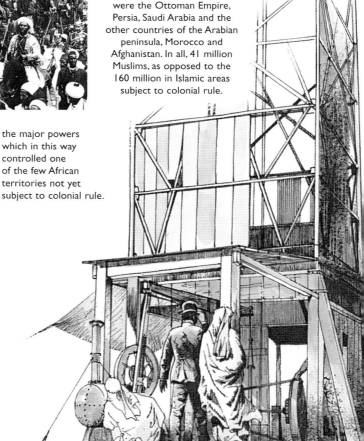

Russians and the English, who they viewed as undermining the autonomy of the empire. The modernists and traditionalists views could not be reconciled, favoring an Anglo-Russian pact and the establishment of a substantial British protectorate over the empire, which only formally retained its independence. This was not the case with Morocco, a territory that France and Spain divided up between them despi-

The Boers
Dutch colonists who in South Africa had created the Orange Free State and the Transvaal at the end of the 19th century. From 1899 to 1902 they fought against the British, who defeated them and founded the Union of South Africa.

te the strong resistance of Berber tribes in the country.

The crisis of the Ottoman Empire

In contrast to Persia and China, in Turkey reform movements were successful in introducing innovative social customs and ways of life. The modernists—the "Young Turks"—provided the state with a liberal constitution, even though this later developed into military dictatorship, and accelerated the final collapse of the tricontinental Ottoman Empire. Military conflicts in the Balkans between 1911 and 1913 deprived the empire of almost all its European possessions, reducing its territory to Anatolia, Middle Eastern regions, Arabia, Yemen and some North African provinces, from which Italy seized Tripolitania and Cyrenaica in 1911.

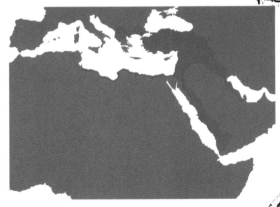

The Ottoman Empire
In 1900 this multi-ethnic empire comprised Albanians, Arabs, Armenians, Bosnians, Bulgarians, Circassians, Greeks, Jews, Kurds, Serbs, Macedonians, and various Turkish peoples.

Mustafa Kemal
A young official belonging to the Young Turks movement. In 1923, after the dissolution of the Ottoman Empire, he became the first president of the Turkish Republic and took the name Ataturk, the "father of the Turks." He conducted a policy of authoritarian modernization in the cities, leaving rural areas in a backward state.

English-style clothes
Western dress was preferred by Turkish modernists.

ISTANBUL
The city was a melting pot of different cultures. The Turkish group that opposed the Sultan subordinated the Islamic religion to the interests of the Turkish nation preferring Western ways and customs to the Arab language and culture.

The Mexican Revolution

In the period that witnessed the dissolution of old and ancient empires, undermined by western colonial and imperial powers and by Japan, the Mexican Revolution appears to be something of a case apart. It may, however, be explained partly by the new state of interdependence among the world's nations. Mexico was an independent state although it was politically and economically dependent on its powerful neighbor, the United States. Here, the first revolution of the twentieth century broke out in 1910, the one in which a people had succeeded in overcoming a regular army and traditional powers.

The long government of General Porfirio Diaz favored the large landowners, who were given lands traditionally available for village peasants,

THE REVOLUTION
It lasted from 1910 to 1917 and saw liberal industrialists and poor peasants united. After the presidency of Francisco Madero, supported by Pancho Villa and Emiliano Zapata, the constitutionalists of Venustiano Carranza prevailed and enacted a limited agrarian reform.

and allowed American and European capital to enter into the country for mercenary activities and the extraction of oil. The revolution of the peasants began in 1910, with the defeat of Diaz, and proceeded with alternating fortunes, and concluded with the granting of a more modern constitution.

Without the support of the United States, preoccupied about the growing economic influence of the British, the Mexican rebels would probably not have known how to organize themselves, nor would the Mexican political revolution have developed without the prolonged intervention of the United States. This presaged an unfortunate characteristic of the century: that conflicts within a weak state have been conditioned by the power interested in that same country.

The leaders of the revolution
Madero, a modernizer, was an industrialist from the North Zapata was the leader of the peasants from the South.

Latin America
Although depending economically on Great Britain and the United States, it modernized its agriculture and developed some light industry from the second half of the 19th century. With the 20th century the dominion of the great landowners continued as did the link between mine owners and British capital. Authoritarian governments remained in office and military coup d'états continued in succession. The arrival of European immigrants modified the cities: in 1914 the population of Buenos Aires numbered a million and a half inhabitants.

THE AGE OF CATASTROPHE: 1914–1945

Thirty years of calamities: two world wars, deportations, horrifying genocides, and a seemingly irremediable economic depression. The world was shaken by waves of rebellion, by a revolution, and by the fight to the death against Nazism.

The genocide of the Armenians

The nineteenth century, after the fall of Napoleon, was characterized in Europe by the absence of total war. There were local and regional conflicts, but these tended to last no more than a few months. This relative peace, which lasted many decades and persisted through the early years of the twentieth century, was shattered in the summer of 1914 when a war broke out that would drag on for four years. This war was initially confined to Europe but later involved the rest of the world, with the intervention of Japan and the United States.

The real prologue to the age of catastrophes, however, was a marginal though no less terrible episode: the deportation and elimination of almost two million Armenians, the first genocide in a century that would, unfortunately, know others. The scene of the tragedy was the Ottoman Empire, the "sick man of Europe," where political weakness undermined a long-established cosmopolitan identity and a traditional tolerance of ethnic and religious groups. The unity of the disintegrating empire was broken by a nationalist movement whose aim was

The spark of the war
On June 28, 1914, Archduke Franz Ferdinand, heir to the Austro-Hungarian empire, was killed in Sarajevo by the Bosnian Serb Gavrilo Princip. Blaming Serbia for this provocation, Austria consequently declared war.

THE ARMENIANS
These Christian people of the Ottoman Empire were almost completely exterminated in various stages between 1894 and 1922.

Invasion of Belgium
Began on August 4, 1914. The German plan was to launch an attack on France through neutral Belgium.

The Eastern Front
In September 1914, at the battle of the Masurian Lakes, the Germans threw back the Russian attack on eastern Prussia. In the photograph Russian soldiers in a Polish city.

The deportation of the Armenians
The Armenians were forced to evacuate the burning villages of eastern Anatolia in 1915 on the pretext of their proximity to the front. During the journey most were killed.

to unite all Turkish people and eliminate the Kurdish and Armenian minorities. Immediately after the outbreak of World War I, when world attention was directed elsewhere, the extermination of the Armenians began.

World War I

The terrible fate of the Armenian people was a tragic expression of the increasingly nationalistic climate that formed the background to the outbreak of war. On June 28, 1914, in Sarajevo, a Serbian nationalist assassinated Austria's crown prince, Archduke Franz Ferdinand, who was visiting the capital of Bosnia-Hercegovina, at that time annexed to Austria but claimed by the Serbs. But domination of the Balkans was only an aspect of the struggle for power that divided the major European powers. Germany, which in the previous fifty years had succeeded in building up a powerful army and navy, now competed with Great Britain for world supremacy.

The conflict began with the declaration of war by Austria and Germany on Serbia. The powers of the Triple Entente—Great Britain, France, and Russia—then entered the war on the side of the Serbs, supported by Montenegro, then Italy, Portugal and Romania, and from 1917 the United States. The alliance of Germany and Austria was supported by the Ottoman Empire and by Bulgaria from 1915.

The two blocs were a manifestation of long-standing European rivalries, rivalries that invariably reflected conflicts of interest in the world's main

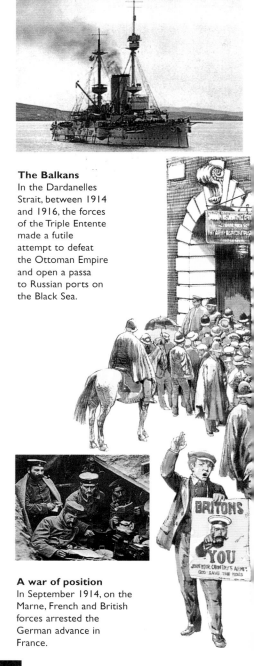

The Balkans
In the Dardanelles Strait, between 1914 and 1916, the forces of the Triple Entente made a futile attempt to defeat the Ottoman Empire and open a passa to Russian ports on the Black Sea.

A war of position
In September 1914, on the Marne, French and British forces arrested the German advance in France.

The war in Africa
Made possible
the British conquest
of German colonies,
but only with
significant losses.

The home front
Support for the war
by many workers' parties
seemed to dissolve the
principles of pacifism
and fraternity of
the organization
known as
the Socialist
International.

**A war of
the masses**
In Europe millions
of peasants were
called to arms. There
were also massive
volunteer enlistments.
In Britain a voluntary
expeditionary corps
was organized and
in London long lines
formed in front
of the recruitment
offices.

colonial areas. In the Balkans, for example, Russia and Austria particularly, even in the face of local nationalist movements, were intent on obtaining a share of the spoils left by the disintegrating Ottoman Empire.

A different kind of war
Both sides expected the war to be over in a few weeks, but this did not happen. A devastating German advance in 1914 was checked by an Allied counter-offensive, and by the end of the year there was stalemate on the Western Front. A totally new type of warfare developed in which the two sides confronted each other along a line of trenches protected by barbed wire and machine guns. It was not always clear who was the victor in major attacks, and even sophisticated new weapons like tanks and poison gas proved ineffective in ending the war. Various huge battles were fought, with horrendous losses on both sides, but they

Infantrymen
Foot soldiers had either repeating rifles, which could shoot 15 rounds a minute, or smaller carbines.

Trenches were dug with spades by soldiers who spent the long years of the war crouching in them. To break the immobility of trench warfare, the English official Ernest Swinton designed the modern tank in 1915.

Radio broadcasts

Wireless communication improved in the years prior to the war, allowing a more efficient coordination of the forces in the field.

The front line
A few months after the beginning of the war the front line consisted of a vast network of trenches. To resist the massive bombardments of artillery that preceded attacks, trenches between 9¾ and 29½ ft. deep were built underground to provide soldiers with temporary refuge.

resulted in no significant territorial changes.

World War I was a war bought by the masses. Soldiers were drawn from all social classes, urged on by propaganda campaigns, and women played an important role behind the lines, especially in guaranteeing the product-

Assault troops
Their job was to cut and blow up barbed wire with explosives.

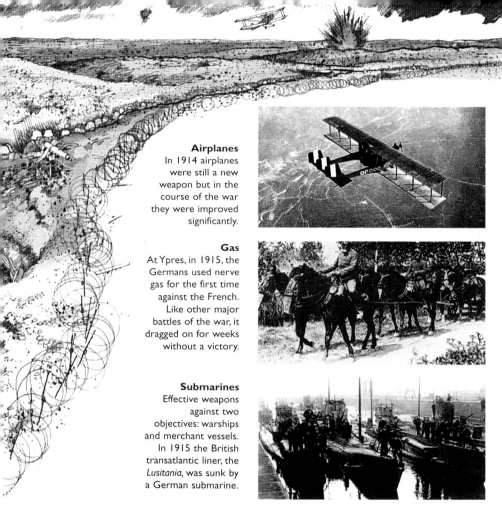

Airplanes
In 1914 airplanes were still a new weapon but in the course of the war they were improved significantly.

Gas
At Ypres, in 1915, the Germans used nerve gas for the first time against the French. Like other major battles of the war, it dragged on for weeks without a victory.

Submarines
Effective weapons against two objectives: warships and merchant vessels. In 1915 the British transatlantic liner, the *Lusitania*, was sunk by a German submarine.

ion of arms. World War I was, therefore, a watershed separating the old world from the new: global involvement, the use of science and new technology and the contribution of millions of men and women were all factors that would continue to characterize the course of human history in the twentieth century.

Russia and the United States

Bitter fighting and huge losses also took place on the Eastern Front, where Russian armies won some early successes against Austria but suffered crushing defeats by the Germans.

As the war dragged on the soldiers became weary of the endless conflict. There were mutinies and desertions in

Great battles
At Verdun, from February 1916, there was a bloodbath between the Germans and French which lasted for ten months. Between July and September, on the Somme, the Allies regained only 4.9 miles.

The naval blockade
The British and German navies sought to impede each other's seaborne supplies by sinking merchant vessels heading for enemy ports. An important battle took place just off the Danish peninsula of Jutland in May 1916.

THE WORK OF WOMEN
During the war women did jobs that would have been unimaginable before the conflict, such as working in factories that produced arms. In Europe, during the war the number of metalworkers increased fivefold.

I WANT YOU FOR U.S. ARMY
NEAREST RECRUITING STATION

American intervention
In April 1917, urged on by public opinion, America entered the war in response to the indiscriminate surface and submarine attacks of the German fleet against convoys heading for England.

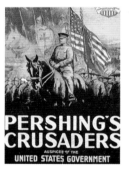

PERSHING'S CRUSADERS
AUSPICES OF THE
UNITED STATES GOVERNMENT

all armies, and executions of insubordinate soldiers multiplied. By 1917 fatigue and suffering were rife on all fronts. This was reflected in the disastrous retreat of the Italian army at Caporetto, which resulted in 31,000 wounded or dead and the taking of 300,000 prisoners. Serious tensions were also registered along the supply lines and in the very heart of society.

In 1917 two new developments were decisive in bringing about an end to the tragedy: the entry into the war of the United States and the Russian Revolution, which paved the way for that country's withdrawal from the war. On April 2, 1917 the United States

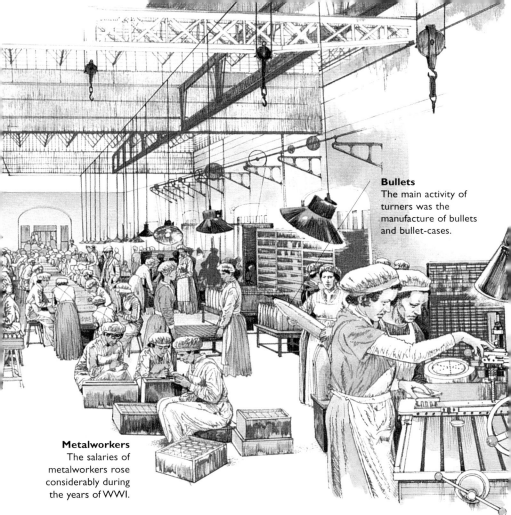

Bullets
The main activity of turners was the manufacture of bullets and bullet-cases.

Metalworkers
The salaries of metalworkers rose considerably during the years of WWI.

declared war on Germany. America's example was almost symbolically followed by Panama, Cuba, Siam, Liberia, China, and Brazil. Almost all the world's continents were now represented in the conflict, a new and unprecedented phenomenon characteristic of the twentieth century.

In December 1917 Russia's new Bolshevik government signed an armistice with Germany, thus allowing German troops to be moved to the Western Front. In March 1918 the Germans launched an offensive that was thrown back in July at the second battle of the Marne. The supreme Allied commander, Marshall Foch, then counterattacked. In the end, between the

The Italian Front
Fighting also took place in mountains that had always been considered too difficult. Italians and Austrians fought in the Eastern Alps between .75 and 1.9 miles.

David Lloyd George
British prime minister

THE PEACE OF VERSAILLES
The peace conference organized by the victorious countries began in January 1919 and was attended by the representatives of 32 states. But real power was held by the leaders of France, Great Britain, and the United States.

Georges Clemenceau
French prime minister

The surrender of the central empires
In the summer of 1918 the war situation suddenly changed. Following the collapse of Austria, the German kaiser abdicated and on November 11, an armistice was signed in a train car.

Vittorio E. Orlando
Italian prime minister

summer and autumn of 1918 the disheartened and demoralized German and Austrian armies surrendered on all fronts.

The peace

All nations welcomed the peace that marked the end to what had seemed a futile and interminable waste of human lives. The terms of the peace were dictated by representatives of the victorious powers, mainly the United States, France, and Great Britain. At the Treaty of Versailles (June 28, 1919) they imposed harsh conditions on the defeated nations. Germany was drastically disarmed and lost much of its territory, especially in the east, as well as its colonies abroad. Germany was also forced to admit its guilt for the damage caused by the war and had to pay reparations.

In many countries the end of the war marked a fundamental transition, the end of the old world of the great imperial dynasties of Germany, Austria-Hungary, Turkey, and Russia. The postwar years were characterized by widespread political breakdown and revolutionary crisis, especially in the defeated states, although social unrest, almost leading to revolution in Italy, was rife even among the victors.

The Russian Revolution of 1917

After the revolts of 1905 the political situation in Russia had remained in a state of precarious equilibrium between the traditional tsarist autocracy and some tentative liberal forms. The peasants were discontented; even its own commanders found the army difficult

Woodrow Wilson
President of the United States

The League of Nations
President Woodrow Wilson promoted the foundation of the new international organization. The League entrusted mandates over the

Ottoman Empire's former Middle-Eastern Arab possessions (outlined in red) to France (in red) and Great Britain (in yellow). The protectorate over Egypt ended in 1922.

to control; growing industrial development reinforced the presence of workers in the cities. The war broke this precarious equilibrium, revealing the dependence of the Russian economy on the West and the poverty of the infrastructures on which the country's economic and commercial life rested. Military defeats during the war had caused humiliation, but paralysis and famine fomented the rebellion.

In February 1917 spontaneous rioting broke out in Petrograd, the capital of the Russian Empire. Strikes and demonstrations had intensified day by day, culminating in a general strike. Troops garrisoned in the city refused orders to fire on the demonstrators and instead joined them. Workers and soldiers elected their own delegates in the city soviet (council), an assembly controlled by an executive committee of professional revolutionaries. Tsar Nicholas II, abandoned by government officials, abdicated in what became known as the February Revolution and a provisional government was established oriented towards the transformation of Russia into a Western-style parliamentary democracy. In the meantime, the war continued, though mutinies were increasingly frequent. Numerous peasant uprisings broke out in many areas.

A small extreme left-wing party, the Bolshevik Party, led by Vladimir Ilyich Lenin, played a decisive role from July. The program Lenin announced on his return from exile was to end the war, establish the power of the soviets (which in the meantime had been set

The Petrograd soviet
Held real power during the crisis of 1917 in which, after the abdication of the tsar and the demonstration of the weakness of the government and army, took control of the situation.

The tsar
Nicholas II Romanov was accused by the Bolsheviks of being responsible for the "Bloody Sunday" massacre of 1905. He was killed with his family in 1918.

Lenin
He ably prepared the revolution in October and once in power imposed the dictatorship of the proletariat or, rather, the Bolshevik Party.

THE BOLSHEVIKS
Obtained growing support because they used the soviet as an organ of power, as opposed to the government, and because they declared their intention to end the war.

up in many other cities), and nationalize the land. On October 25 (November 7 for the Western calendar) the Bolsheviks, with the support of the army, seized the Winter Palace, the seat of the provisional government. On the following day Lenin proclaimed the dictatorship of the proletariat.

The Russian Revolution was the first socialist revolution in history. But it did not happen as had been predicted in the nineteenth century by the founder of scientific socialism, the German-born Jewish philosopher Karl Marx. Marx believed that the first such revolution would happen in an advanced industrialized country. In such a society—according to Marx—the maintenance of the private property of the material means of production inhibited the development and growth of well-being. This, in turn, made necessary the collectivization of the means of production.

Russia was a backward country. After the peace of 1918 and at the end of

USSR
(Union of Soviet Socialist Republics)
Industrialization was accelerated and in the countryside peasants were forced to pool their own resources in large collective farms.

The kulaks
Millions of land-owning peasants, called kulaks, were either deported or executed and their properties were confiscated.

the war in Europe, it was also an isolated country that the democratic governments of the world regarded with suspicion and hostility. In spite of the growing force of socialist parties in post-war Europe, particularly Germany, the proletarian revolution did not take place in any other country. Russia's tsarist empire was transformed into a republic, the USSR, still a great multi-ethnic country that covered a sixth of the world's land. The new Soviet state embarked on an ambitious program of industrialization that involved enormous sacrifices and hardship for people in rural areas and the peasants. After Lenin's death in 1924, the new party secretary, Josif Stalin, put into operation his plans to develop heavy industry (arms, machinery) and force collectivization of rural areas. He violently suppressed his political rivals and between 1936 and 1939 began a reign of terror, using trials which ended in death sentences as an instrument of mass education.

Odessa
Ships at the port of this developing industrial city were loaded with grain, the only means Russia had to pay for the machinery purchased in the West that was indispensable for industrialization.

Immigration to the city
Many millions of peasants deserted the countryside to work in heavy industries in the cities.

Stalin
Josif Dzhugashvili, known as Stalin, freed himself of all political rivals and transformed Russia, with force and at the cost of millions of lives, into an industrialized country.

THE GREAT DEPRESSION
Began in 1929. Among its causes
was an over-production of goods
compared to purchasing capacity.
Countries exporting foodstuffs
could no longer exchange
their production with that
of industrialized countries.
Huge reserves accumulated.

The reduction of international trade

Between 1929 and 1931 world trade diminished by a third. Many countries came off the gold standard, the system of convertibility between currencies and gold.

The Empire State Building

With its height of 1,250 feet it was for decades the highest building in the world. Although built after the outbreak of the crisis, it was the symbol of the opulent 1920s in America.

Crisis in Europe

In England and Germany violent social conflicts exploded. Hunger and poverty became widespread throughout Europe, though far more dramatic was the situation in Germany where conditions were increasingly ripe for the advent of Nazism.

Coffee

The staple product of the Brazilian economy. Unsold surpluses were used to fuel locomotives.

The Great Depression

In Russia the forced collectivization of rural areas was a failure. Nevertheless, with the force of industrialization, accompanied by a strong commitment to education, the USSR made a gigantic productive leap forward between 1929 and 1940. Russia's tyrannical leader, Stalin, aimed to remove the backwardness that had led the tsarist empire to centuries-old defeat.

At the same time the economy of the West, from the prosperity of the 1920s, went into a shattering decline. To understand the cause of this phenomenon, remember that the world economy was increasingly integrated. What happened in one important part of the world economy had repercussions in all other regions. After the end of World War I the United States dominated the world economy, not just because of the enormous development in production and social well-being, but also because the United States was the world's bank. American capital was present throughout Europe. France, for example, believed it could pay off its own foreign debt by cashing in on the heavy reparations that the peace treaty of 1918 had imposed on Germany. But it was American money that sustained the German economy. During the 1920s America went through a great period of prosperity that allowed a major expansion of trade and world production, revealing the interrelationship of an increasingly integrated global economy. But it was precisely the boom in production that made it impossible for people to buy everything that was being produced by the industrial system. Two phenomena emerge: the overproduction of goods compared to the demand of buyers and the movement of money towards financial speculation.

The New York Stock Exchange provided the mechanism for investors to put their money into company shares. Here, in October 1929 a disastrous fall occurred in the value of share prices.

The effects of the crash were devastating. Thousands of investors were ruined. American overseas loans were withdrawn, so that European countries were pushed into a depression. Investors who had bought shares with credit were now called upon to pay cash, which they could only do by selling at much lower prices. Industrial

FIGHTING THE DEPRESSION
In March 1933 Franklin Delano Roosevelt became president of the United States. He launched a campaign, the "new deal," against unemployment and economic paralysis.

production slumped, factories shut down, businesses were ruined, shops went bankrupt, banks closed, and unemployment rose. The Great Depression had begun. The prices of raw materials fell drastically and food-stuffs produced by many countries in the world remained unsold.

The crisis appeared to be unfixable, although it wasn't. But certainly the Great Depression had profound effects on the future course of the twentieth century.

The New Deal
The results of the New Deal were quite remarkable, and for the first time there had been cooperation between the government and society to regulate the market and stimulate development.

Roosevelt and the New Deal

The immediate answer to the crisis was a change in American policy from 1933 promoted by the nation's new president, Franklin Delano Roosevelt. Roosevelt inspired great faith in the American people, who were reassured by his honest, hard-working, and common-sense approach to the social and economic crisis. He promised Americans a "New Deal," introducing reforms that gave the government more power in running the country. He put banks under federal control in order to restore people's confidence in them. Various agencies were set up to provide useful work for the unemployed, and farmers were helped with government incentives. Other reforms ensured better working conditions, unemploy-ment benefit, and old-age pensions.

The reforms of the New Deal contributed to the revival of the American economy, but the real end to the Depression came only with World War II, when rearmament and the international demand for arms boosted

The Tennessee Valley Authority
Under the Roosevelt presidency, in 1933, one of the greatest examples of social planning in the United States was enacted: a federal organization was charged with planning and building a complex of works whose aim was the reclamation of the Tennessee Valley.

industry, and full employment and prosperity returned.

Hitler and Nazism

In 1921 Adolf Hitler became the leader of the National Socialist German Workers' Party, the Nazi Party, which gained widespread support after 1930 when the Great Depression hit Germany and produced millions of unemployed. Through an efficient propaganda machine, Hitler's Nazi ideas reached a mass audience and became popular especially with the middle classes and the young, who were impressed by the dynamism of the Nazi movement and its charismatic leader. Hitler called for the rejection of the Versailles Treaty and

The persecution of the Jews

A priority of the regime of Hitler, who accused the Jews of conspiring against the state. First their activities were boycotted, then their citizenship was denied, which forced some of them to leave their own country, while others became the target of unemployment and persecution.

Nazi rallies

Germany's policy of rearmament had created employment and therefore had won people's approval of the regime. Huge spectacular rallies celebrated Nazi power and exalted its popularity.

the rebirth of Germany. He also called for the unity of the German people, who, he declared, were a superior "Aryan race." Hitler blamed the Jews and later persecuted them for most of the ills affecting Germany. Ably out-maneuvering his political rivals, Hitler finally took control of all institutions and gained the support of the army. In

The sarcasm of Charlie Chaplin

In 1940 one of the greatest geniuses in the history of the cinema made the film The Great Dictator, a stinging caricature of the megalomania of Adolf Hitler.

1934 he became Führer of the German Reich, the leader of a totalitarian Nazi state under his personal dictatorship.

Freedom movements

By the second half of the nineteenth century the economy of Western countries had penetrated almost all areas of the globe. Consequently, the Great Depression of 1929–1933 strongly affected political life and independence movements in many areas of the world. Colonial countries supplied raw materials for industry and energy production, as well as agricultural and livestock products. To make their colonial possessions functional the

Japan
Under the pressure of the world economic crisis, the military reacted by increasing their political power and attacked China with the invasion of Manchuria in 1931.

ruling powers invested resources in the form of loans and in communications systems and other services.

In the 1930s industry was a Western monopoly. Japan was the only exception which, besides promoting its own increasingly consolidated industrialization, spread the system of industrial production into Korea, Manchuria, and Taiwan, in the colonies subject to its growing dominion.

In countries under colonial rule nationalist movements were small and usually led by a Western-educated elite. These groups had two objectives: to modernize the country and to mobilize their more traditional fellow countrymen against the colonial power. The

Mao Tse Tung
In 1934, in response to attacks carried out by the Chinese Nationalist government of Chiang Kai-shek, Mao led 100,000 Communists on the "Long March," a dramatic 5,593 mile journey across China.

GANDHI
India's spiritual leader who won the hearts of his people. In 1930 he organized a march of 236 miles to affirm the right of Indians to extract salt in protest against the English government's monopoly.

alliance between the elite and the people was difficult mainly because the Asian and African masses were generally conservative in outlook.

There was, however, a great exception in India: a man who committed himself to the freedom of his people, mediating between the values of Muslim and Hindu cultures without abandoning his own convictions as a modernizer. His name was Mohandas Karamchand Gandhi. Gandhi, how-

The Axum stele
Like the ancient Romans, who were a great inspiration to Fascism, the Italians brought an African obelisk to Rome.

THE ETHIOPIAN EMPIRE
One of the four independent states in Africa until Italian Fascist aggression in 1935. The other three were Liberia (from 1847), The Republic of South Africa (1910), and Egypt (1922).

Fascism
Fascism showed its expansionist face in Ethiopia. Immediately after the invasion of Ethiopia and its condemnation by the League of Nations, Italy came closer to Germany, also adopting its anti-Semitic policy.

ever, was an extreme example, not only a person endowed with a great spirituality, a man who appeared saint like, but also a political leader who operated with a highly original instrument: nonviolent resistance.

Struggle in Europe
The participation of one million Indians in World War I did not at the time seem to have any great political significance. But in Europe profound social and political repercussions followed the entry of peasants and workers on the historical landscape. In Italy, frustration over the treatment received in the Treaty of Versailles, and the weakness of the liberal and industrial tradition, gave rise to a vast movement of the middle class masses, strongly inspired by nationalist ideals. This movement became the Fascist Party. The common interests of the great industrialists of the north and the landowners of the center and south led the movement to seize power in 1922. The Fascists created a totalitarian state founded on such right-wing values as authoritarianism and extreme nationalism.

The expansionist aims of the Fascist leader, Benito Mussolini, who was soon taken as a model by Hitler himself, prompted Italy to conquer a colony. In 1936 Italy invaded Ethiopia, thus suppressing the sovereignty of the last of the ancient African kingdoms that had remained independent.

The Italian aggression was strongly criticized by all the other European colonial powers. Ethiopia was a member of the League of Nations, the international organization founded by

Fascism
In the 1930s, following the example of Mussolini and Hitler, right-wing authoritarian regimes came to power in Portugal, Spain, the Balkans, Austria, Romania, Hungary, Poland, the Baltic, Greece and Turkey.

President Woodrow Wilson after World War I. The inability of the League to guarantee the fundamental rights of a member state clearly revealed its powerlessness. In fact, by the time the USSR had become a member of the League in 1934, Germany and Japan had already left it. The world, therefore, was without an international institution capable of guaranteeing peace. In Europe and in the world this era brought the emergence of two opposing power blocs, western democracies and the Communist USSR against Fascism.

The Spanish Civil War

The rebellion of the right-wing Spanish general Francisco Franco against the legitimate government of the Frente

Italians and Germans
The Germans sent mainly their air force. Italian Fascists supported Franco, while Italian anti-Fascists sided with the legitimate government of the Popular Front.

Francisco Franco
On July 17, 1936, Franco rose with his garrison against the government of the democratic parties that had won the elections in February.

Soviet advisers
They carefully observed the presence of the Communists in the government, the first example of its kind in western Europe.

FRENTE POPULAR
The coalition between socialists, anarchists, and communists which had won the elections of 1925.

Popular, which had won the elections of 1936, dragged the new republic of Spain, which had remained neutral in 1914–1918, into a bloody civil war that ended with the victory of Franco and the establishment of a new totalitarian regime in Europe. Men of other countries also fought in the Spanish Civil War. It was the first international armed conflict between Fascists and

The International Brigades
In support of the legitimate government, these volunteers were formed of anti-

Fascists from all over the world. In addition to the Italian anti-Fascists, there were French, Belgians, English, Germans, and Americans.

Art and war
Guernica is the name of a Spanish village that was bombarded by the German Air

Force. In 1937, the great painter Pablo Picasso dedicated a famous painting to this tragedy.

The great intellectuals
The American writer Ernest Hemingway participated in the anti-Fascist struggle to which he dedicated the novel *For Whom the Bell Tolls*. The Spanish poet Federíco García Lorca was killed by the Fascists in Granada in 1936.

anti-Fascists, an ominous forewarning of the now imminent World War II.

Important new developments

Following the scientific breakthroughs in the natural sciences and psychology that marked the beginning of the century, a great leap forward occurred in our knowledge of human society. Even before Western nations ceased to rule that part of the world they had colonized, western culture became aware of the salve of differences between cultures and their equal dignity. This amounted to the Europeans renouncing the idea that their way of thinking was valid for all people.

Research carried out between 1925 and 1939 in Polynesia and New Guinea by the American anthropologist Margaret Mead showed how twentieth-century western culture was now questioning the foundations of its centuries-old ethnographic supremacy. While ethnological studies criticized western prejudices and validated the customs of different cultures, new

THE REVIVAL OF CULTURE

Overwhelmed by global war and revolutions the world no longer appeared easy to understand. Just as Freud had penetrated the human unconscious, the human and social sciences aimed to explore the cultural identity of different societies. Ethnology, in particular, set out to study peoples who until then had been considered savage.

Max Weber

German scholar living in the late 19th and early 20th century who studied the social and religious origins of capitalism. His work was an example of the growing interest in the social sciences in the 20th century.

In Samoa

Margaret Mead, an ethnographer, published a book in 1929 on the adolescent life of Samoan women that generated considerable interest in the United States.

developments in physics and astrophysics enabled twentieth-century men and women to form ideas about the universe that differed radically from those of past centuries.

At the end of the 1920s the American astronomer Edwin Hubble discovered that the galaxies around us were moving farther away from our own. By measuring the distances between different galaxies, he concluded that the more distant galaxies were moving away faster than the nearer ones. Hubble's laws of physics tell us, then, that the whole universe is expanding in all directions at high speed.

These discoveries led to new ideas about the origin of the universe and gave rise to a heated scientific debate between supporters and opponents of the "Big Bang" theory and the concept of the steady state.

At a simpler level, the progress of science and technology was transforming life-styles from the 1920s. This

The Big Bang
According to the most widely accepted theory, fifteen billion years ago a gigantic explosion led to the beginning of universe, space, and time.

2. Between 10^{-36} and 10^{-32} secs. the universe expands at amazing speed.

Albert Einstein
A German citizen, Einstein was forced to emigrate to the United States. He worked on the American atomic program but later took a stand against the threat that atomic weapons represented.

3. 10^{-32} secs.: formation of the first elementary particles (quarks).

Edwin Hubble
An American astronomer, considered to be the greatest cosmologist of the 20th century. From the idea of the expanding universe derived the conclusion that far back in time there was a moment when the entire universe was contained in a very small space.

I. Between 10^{-43} and 10^{-36} secs. the four principal forces separate: gravity, strong nuclear, electromagnetics, and weak nuclear.

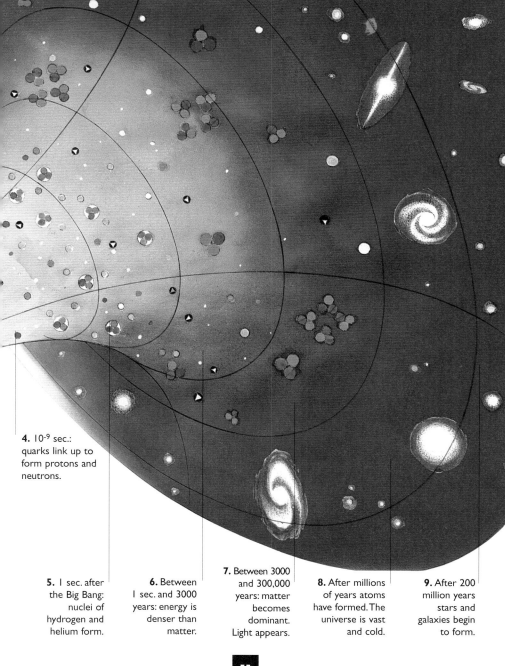

4. 10^{-9} sec.: quarks link up to form protons and neutrons.

5. 1 sec. after the Big Bang: nuclei of hydrogen and helium form.

6. Between 1 sec. and 3000 years: energy is denser than matter.

7. Between 3000 and 300,000 years: matter becomes dominant. Light appears.

8. After millions of years atoms have formed. The universe is vast and cold.

9. After 200 million years stars and galaxies begin to form.

MOVIES

Created one evening in 1895. Between the 1910s and the 1960s it was the most popular and influential form of entertainment and means of mass communication.

SURREALISM

An artistic movement that aspired to the inner freedom of the individual. On January 7, 1938 the International Exhibition of Surrealism opened in Paris. The public was attracted by the paradoxical and magical themes and juxtapositions presented by Salvador Dalí and other artists.

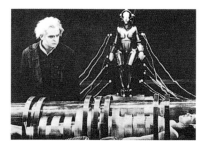

Metropolis

In a megalopolis of the 21st century conflicts break out between the dictator and the workers. The film, one of the most impressive in the story of the cinema, was made by the German director Fritz Lang.

Modern Times

Charlot, Charlie Chaplin, who has gone insane as a result of the heavy and repetitive pace of work in the factory, is the protagonist of this modern fable of 1936.

Walt Disney

Snow White and the Seven Dwarfs of 1938 marked a turning-point in the story of the cinema. In this full-length film production, the world of fantasy reached unprecedented heights.

Jazz

In New York, in the 1920s, the district of Harlem became the cultural capital of African-Americans. The celebrated Duke Ellington, one of the greatest performers of jazz, the music created by African-Americans in the 20th century, played at the famous Cotton Club.

Magic cave Marcel Duchamp had the central hall transformed into a sort of fabulous grotto: 1200 sacks of coal hung from the ceiling.

Salvador Dalí At the entrance to the exhibition Dalí placed a taxi in which two dummies were continually being hit by water.

transformation was especially evident with the establishment of a new culture of sound and vision through cinema, radio, and new musical styles like jazz. Advertising spread in new popular daily newspapers and illustrated magazines.

The spirit of modernism dominated styles in literature, art, and architecture. The catastrophic years earlier in the century showed none of the same innovativeness of the artistic avant-garde. The surrealist and constructivist movements were its most original expressions.

World War II

World War II (1939–1945) was above all a conflict in which the great majority of governments and peoples put aside their differences and united against a common enemy, Nazism. Nazism was an aggressive force that did not hesitate to commit crimes against humanity in order to rise to world power. Attempts at diplomacy in the late 1930s proved futile and in September 1939, following Hitler's invasion of Poland, Britain and France declared war on Germany. Later the Allies would be supported by the USSR and the United States, while Nazi Germany received the support of Fascist Italy and later Japan.

In 1940 Germany unleashed the full might of its military machine in lightning warfare tactics. In just two months Denmark, Norway, the Netherlands, and Belgium were overrun. France was also invaded and called for an armistice. Under its terms all of northern France was occupied by the Germans, while the rest was ruled by a puppet French government at Vichy. In the Battle of Britain the British Air Force successfully resisted German aggression. British troops were also responsible for early Allied victories over Italian forces in North Africa.

In the spring of 1941 Hitler invaded the Soviet Union with 3 million men. Despite its initial successes the German advance was checked before the onset of winter.

In Africa the brilliant desert warfare of General Rommel revived the fortunes of the Germans and Italians. The British were pushed out of Libya and driven back to Egypt.

At the end of the year Japan attacked the main base of the American Pacific

The beginning of the war
On September 1, 1939 five German divisions invaded Poland while airplanes of the Luftwaffe bombarded Warsaw.

FROM THE WAR ROOM
In a specially equipped bunker the British High Command directed operations with the most sophisticated communications technology.

The German advance
By June 1940 Hitler had
arrived in Paris: at this
point only Great Britain
opposed Germany.

War in the air
The German bombing
"blitz" of London claimed
thousands of victims, but
failed to lower the morale
of the British people.

**The defense of
Britain**
This was ensured
thanks to the pilots
of the Royal Air
Force and to radar.
On September 7,
1940 a massive
attack of the German
Air Force was
pushed back.
On September 17,
the Germans
abandoned "Sea
Lion," the planned
invasion of Britain.

Fleet at Pearl Harbor, in Hawaii. In the space of a few months the Japanese seized control of vast areas of the Pacific and Southeast Asia, from Burma and Malaysia to the Philippines and New Guinea.

In 1942 the fortunes of war began to change in favor of the Allied forces. In Africa, at the battle of El Alamein, the British under Montgomery broke Rommel's offensive towards the Suez Canal, while some French troops in Africa refused to respond to the Nazi-

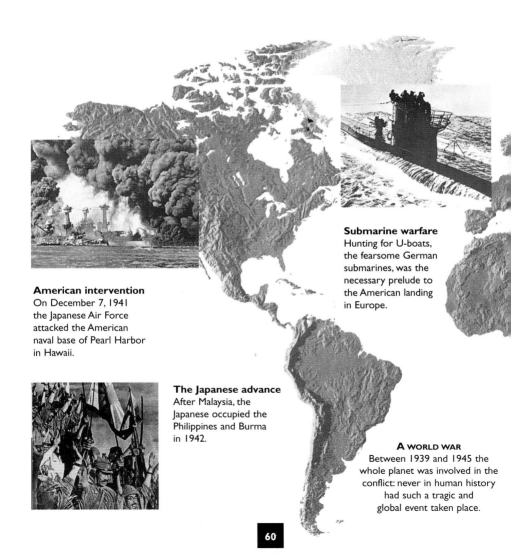

Submarine warfare
Hunting for U-boats, the fearsome German submarines, was the necessary prelude to the American landing in Europe.

American intervention
On December 7, 1941 the Japanese Air Force attacked the American naval base of Pearl Harbor in Hawaii.

The Japanese advance
After Malaysia, the Japanese occupied the Philippines and Burma in 1942.

A WORLD WAR
Between 1939 and 1945 the whole planet was involved in the conflict: never in human history had such a tragic and global event taken place.

friendly government in France and sided with the Allies.

Between November 1942 and February 1943 the Germans suffered a decisive defeat by the Russians at the battle of Stalingrad. This was a turning point that marked the beginning of Germany's long retreat from the Eastern Front.

In July 1943 British and American forces invaded Sicily. Mussolini's Fascist government was dismissed by the Italian king, and Italy withdrew from the war. To counter the Allied advance

The invasion of Russia
On June 22, 1941 the Germans unleashed an attack on the Soviet Union, whose defenses, taken by surprise, were overwhelmed.

War in the desert
Its leading figure was the German general Rommel, known as the "Desert Fox," who had been sent to Africa by Hitler to make up for Italian losses at the hands of the British.

Above the Pacific
In a great air battle in May 1942 the Americans defeated the Japanese Air Force.

from the south the Germans occupied Italy, removing troops from the coastal defense of France. In the meantime the Americans counter-attacked Japanese positions in the Pacific.

On June 6, 1944 (D-Day) British and American forces landed in Normandy, and France once again became a theater of war. The Allies, aided by the French Resistance, drove the Germans back and in August recaptured Paris. France had been freed. Meanwhile, in the Far East, Burma was taken from the Japanese and, island after island, the Americans advanced in the Pacific.

From the winter of 1944 the Allies prepared their final assault against Hitler. On the Western Front the Germans were pushed back to the Rhine, while in April 1945 British and American forces entered Milan, which had already been freed by a popular insurrection. The activities of the Italian Resistance redeemed Italy from its original participation in the war on the side of Hitler.

On the Eastern Front Stalin's Red Army advanced inexorably across

The Final Solution
In July 1941 the Nazi high official Goering issued orders to come to the "final solution" of the "Jewish Question": all Jews in the occupied territories were to be deported and then killed.

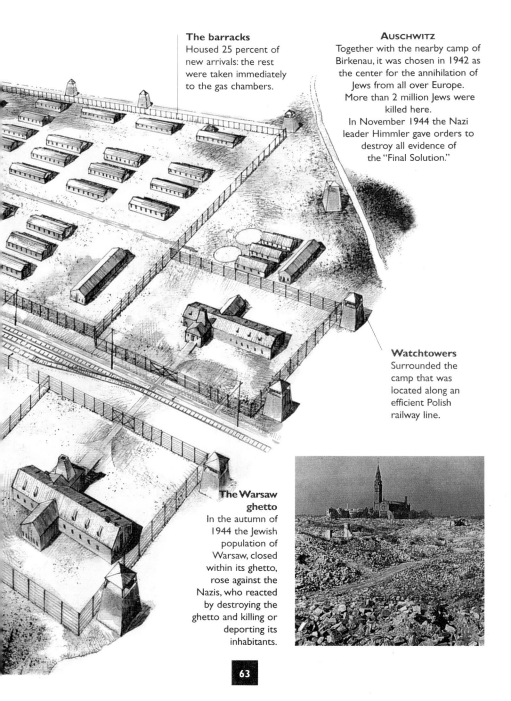

The barracks
Housed 25 percent of new arrivals: the rest were taken immediately to the gas chambers.

AUSCHWITZ
Together with the nearby camp of Birkenau, it was chosen in 1942 as the center for the annihilation of Jews from all over Europe. More than 2 million Jews were killed here.
In November 1944 the Nazi leader Himmler gave orders to destroy all evidence of the "Final Solution."

Watchtowers
Surrounded the camp that was located along an efficient Polish railway line.

The Warsaw ghetto
In the autumn of 1944 the Jewish population of Warsaw, closed within its ghetto, rose against the Nazis, who reacted by destroying the ghetto and killing or deporting its inhabitants.

The turning point of the war

The German advance was halted on February 2, 1943 in Stalingrad, when fieldmarshal Von Paulus, with 90,000 Germans, surrendered to the Red Army. From this moment the Russians were on the offensive.

The Normandy landings

On June 6, 1944 a fleet of over 5,000 ships, with troops and amphibious craft, appeared just off the coast of Normandy. For the Germans it meant fighting on another front besides the Eastern one.

THE ULTIMATE LIE

The Jews were told that they would be taken to the showers. Instead what awaited them were the gas chambers and then the cremation ovens. The image of a smoking chimney is one of the most tragically famous of the Holocaust.

 central and eastern Europe and the Balkans towards Berlin. In Russia, Poland, and Yugoslavia the work of the Resistance was crucial to the defeat of the retreating German army.

In February 1945 the British prime minister Winston Churchill, Stalin, and Roosevelt met in Yalta in the Crimea to decide on arrangements to be made after the war ended in Germany, Poland, and the Far East.

In April the Russians took Vienna, and in May, following the fall of Berlin and Hitler's suicide, the Germans surrendered unconditionally. At the end of the year an international tribunal was set up in the German city of Nuremberg, which tried and condemned some of the surviving leading Nazi war criminals.

World War II was more devastating than World War I, claiming the lives of approximately 20 million Russians, 10 million Chinese, 5 million Germans, 2 million Japanese, an incalculable number of Poles who were massacred en mass by the Nazis and the Russians, and several more million Europeans and Americans.

The Holocaust

Anti-semitic feeling was apparent in the twentieth century with varying intensity even before the World War I, particularly in Russia, but also in France. In the 1920s anti-Semitism increased in Germany, where Jews were blamed and hated for Germany's defeat and humiliation in the war. Hitler held a deeply anti-Semitic belief that the Jews were

The liberation of Paris
On August 26, 1944, after four years of German occupation, Paris was freed, and Charles De Gaulle was recognized as leader of the legitimate French government.

The conquest of Berlin
In April 1945 the Red Army look the capital city of the Reich. On May 8 Germany surrendered.

Iwo Jima
On February 19, 1945 Americans conquered the island with the loss of 6,000 marines. It was the first Allied landing in Japanese territory.

THE RESISTANCE
The armed resistance of civilian men and women in occupied countries was one of the most glorious chapters in the Second World War. Italian resistance against the occupying Nazi forces, after the fall of Fascism, was a particularly heartfelt liberation.

Propaganda
One of the main objectives of the Resistance. Secretly printed leaflets were distributed in workplaces, urging people to rise against the Nazis.

Secrecy
Partisans worked under cover even in the heart of the cities, despite the careful vigilance of the Nazis. Their strengths were surprise actions and the support of the population.

simply unfit to live. When he came to power he promoted a campaign to eliminate them from society. The culmination of Nazi anti-Semitism came during the World War II, when an estimated 6 million Jews were exterminated in concentration camps. This mass murder—known as the Holocaust, or "Shoah"—was one of the most terrible of the entire century.

The atomic age

Even after the defeat of Germany in May 1945, war continued in the Far East. On July 26, 1945 the American and Chinese governments demanded Japan's immediate surrender, warning of terrible destruction if their ultimatum was not met. On August 6 and 8, two atomic bombs were dropped on the Japanese cities of Hiroshima and Nagasaki, killing 200,000 people. This was followed by Japan's unconditional surrender on September 2.

Atomic physics was not merely responsible for contributing to the end of World War II, but also represented a fundamental change in the concept of science itself. The Manhattan Project, launched to develop the atomic bomb, marked the transition from "little science" to "big science," from the work of individual scientists to large teams of scientists working together, with a colossal expansion in all areas of research. At Los Alamos, New Mexico, the U.S. government set up a

Yalta

British leader Churchill, American president Roosevelt, and Russian leader Stalin met in Yalta to decide on the new world order after the war. Each of them would have influence in the areas their armies had occupied.

LOS ALAMOS

The first scientists entrusted with the building of the atomic bomb began to arrive in the desert of New Mexico in 1943. In July, Los Alamos had 1900 inhabitants. At the end of 1944 its population had risen to 6000. Later the laboratories extended to become a veritable city for scientists, technicians, and the military.

Key

 Old area

 Technical area

 Residential area

 Military area

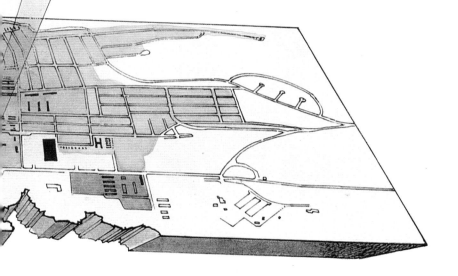

special establishment for nuclear research, where scientific and engineering skills were combined with the aim of improving military technology. This interaction between science, technology, and the construction of increasingly sophisticated weapons would play a prominent role in the balance of world power throughout the rest of the century.

The new order

In the final stages of the war the Allied commanders had frequently met to establish not only military strategy but also the future world order after the Nazis had been defeated. After an initial meeting in Teheran in 1943, it was at Yalta that the fortunes of the post-war world were decided. Finally, at Potsdam, in the summer of 1945, the new American president Truman accepted the principle that each victorious nation would control the territories freed by its army. Thus, the USSR would dominate the countries of Eastern Europe (Hungary, Poland, Czechoslovakia, Bulgaria, Romania and, for a short time, Yugoslavia and Albania). Germany was divided into two states: the Federal Republic in the west, and the Democratic Republic in the east under Soviet influence. Western Europe looked to the United States for its leadership, the USSR dominated Eastern Europe, and the rest of the world allied with one or the other of the two superpowers or professed neutrality.

1¼ miles away
Clothes and laundry hanging out caught fire spontaneously. Everything within this radius burned.

At the center of the explosion
Vertically above the explosion the temperature reached 7232°F, enough to melt the quartz components in granite and the clay of roof tiles.

2½ miles away
There were survivors but their skin was severely burned. At this distance the shock wave was still so strong that it swept away tiles and small objects.

THE ATOM BOMB

Dropped from a height of 1,900 ft. on the center of the Japanese town of Hiroshima at 8:15 on the morning of August 6, 1945. In an instant, the explosion reduced the city to a wasteland. It is estimated that the deaths, either caused directly or as a result of radiation, numbered over 140,000.

THE GOLDEN AGE: 1946–1972

The Age of Catastrophe was followed by thirty years of economic growth and social transformation. The balance resulting from the terror of nuclear weapons prevented World War III, while entire continents began to break free of Western rule.

Unprecedented development

At the end of the most devastating war in recorded history, a phase of exceptional growth of the world economy began. Between 1946 and 1973 the production of foodstuffs and industrial goods, per capita income, and world population increased in a way that had no precedent in history.

As they started down the road to reconstruction, the governments and people of developed countries vividly recalled the catastrophe and its causes, which were seen mainly as the great financial and economic crisis that preceded World War II. The international nature of the economy had led some countries to seek a possible solution in protectionism, the limiting of foreign exchange. The limits and failures of a market without checks or controls had become evident and there was

Reconstruction
In 1944, at Bretton Woods in New Hampshire, the representatives of 44 countries met and instituted the International

Monetary Fund (IMF), the return to the monetary system based on the gold standard: the dollar, an international currency, could be exchanged with gold.

The dollar
The system established at Bretton Woods functioned on the strength of the American economy. The United States

became the world's major creditor. The United States benefited when world currency was stable since they guaranteed its loans.

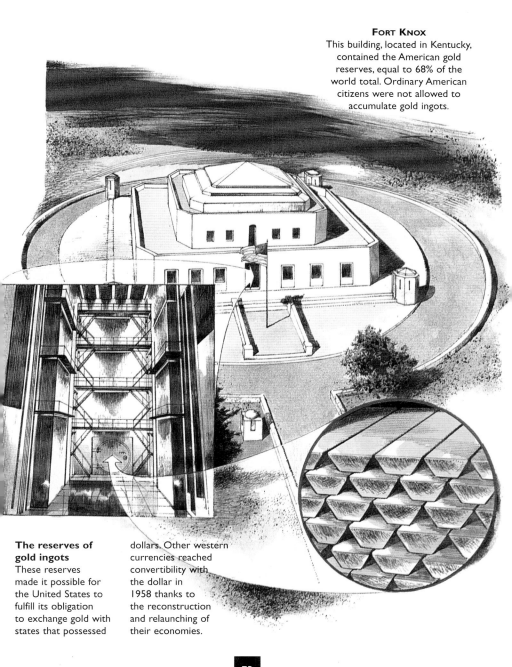

The reserves of gold ingots
These reserves made it possible for the United States to fulfill its obligation to exchange gold with states that possessed dollars. Other western currencies reached convertibility with the dollar in 1958 thanks to the reconstruction and relaunching of their economies.

growing awareness that mass unemployment could pose serious obstacles to industrial development and generate political instability. Between the two wars, Great Britain, former leader of the world economy, had lost its guiding role and now showed the weakness of its production and financial structures.

At the end of World War II, the world's strongest country economically and financially, the United States, appeared to be in a position to finance the relaunching of the European and Japanese economies. Post-war reconstruction was founded on this premise. Growth became a world phenomenon. In the most heavily industrialized economies, increased production, intensified international trade, and growing employment created the conditions for greater wealth. Meanwhile, the world's population grew by leaps and bounds in Africa, South and East Asia, and even more so in Latin America. For the first time in history, a rapid growth in population was not followed by famine: the production of foodstuffs grew faster than population. Until the 1970s, this trend stayed relatively steady. Historians attribute this primarily to two phenomena: the reorganization of the means of capitalist production and the growing internationalization of the economy.

How do we define reorganization of the means of production? After the war, throughout the West, leaders were increasing aware of the serious consequences threatening the economy, and

The communist world
In the 1950s the growth rates of the economies of the Soviet Union and the countries of eastern Europe were higher than those of western countries.

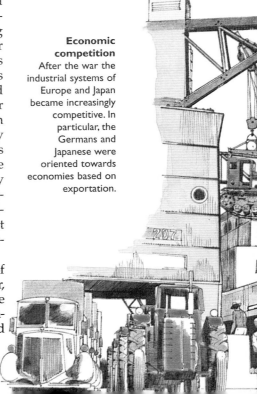

Economic competition
After the war the industrial systems of Europe and Japan became increasingly competitive. In particular, the Germans and Japanese were oriented towards economies based on exportation.

IN THE GOLDEN AGE
International trade was one of
the main factors contributing to
prosperity. The GATT agreements
(General Agreement on Tariffs
and Trade) of 1947 reduced the
obstacles to world trade, like
customs dues.

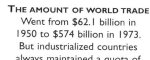

THE AMOUNT OF WORLD TRADE
Went from $62.1 billion in
1950 to $574 billion in 1973.
But industrialized countries
always maintained a quota of
two-thirds of sales,
and trade developed mainly
among them.

**The automobile
industry**
After the middle
of the 1960s, the
German automobile
industry, together
with many others,
operated in Latin
America, Africa,
and Southeast
Asia. The new
industries supplied
not only the home
markets but also
the world one.

especially democracy, if the system of industrial production was left completely in the hands of private interests, with no government control. In other words, it became necessary for the government to plan and direct important aspects of the economy: it had to intervene in defining what needed to be produced and, either partially or entirely, it had to own the companies it empowered to manage such strategic areas as communications and the supply and development of energy resources.

It was by now obvious to politicians, economists, and industrialists that a balance was needed between an increase in the production of goods and the earnings of the members of society, between the quantity of goods produced and the capacity of consumers to purchase them.

THE DECREASE IN THE AGRICULTURAL POPULATION In the West this trend was accompanied by growth in production at the rate of 2 to 4 percent a year. The most remarkable progress was made in the United States due to the availability of land, mechanization, and motorization. An American farmer fed 4 people in 1860, 12 in 1940, and 60 in 1990.

Cereals
The staple food of most of the world's population. In some parts of the world productivity was increased with new crops and fertilizers. But in western Africa the annual increase after the war was much lower than in Asia. Drought and the inadequacy of services forced many countries to rely on food supplies from abroad (photograph).

Workers' wages, in turn, had to be regulated by the balance between an increase in the sales of goods and the need to maintain profits, that is, the earnings of the entrepreneurial class. The most widespread theories claimed that in a society tending towards the full employment of its work force, it was the workers themselves who guaranteed the absorption of the goods they could purchase, thanks to the rise in their salaries and their improved standard of living.

The international character of the Western economy was based on the determination, shared by all countries, to increase production, boost foreign

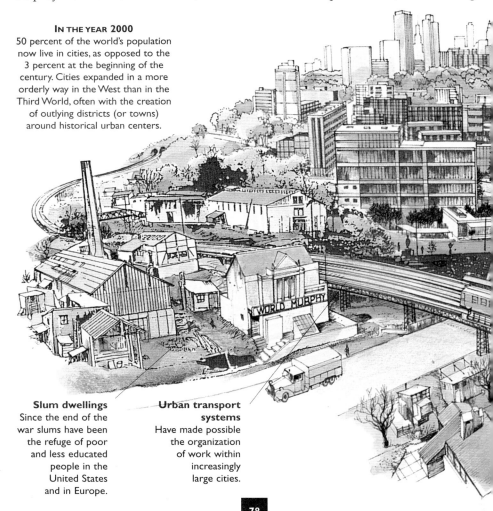

IN THE YEAR 2000
50 percent of the world's population now live in cities, as opposed to the 3 percent at the beginning of the century. Cities expanded in a more orderly way in the West than in the Third World, often with the creation of outlying districts (or towns) around historical urban centers.

Slum dwellings
Since the end of the war slums have been the refuge of poor and less educated people in the United States and in Europe.

Urban transport systems
Have made possible the organization of work within increasingly large cities.

trade, attain full employment, and industrialize and modernize the world. Development was possible because of the supremacy of the United States, such international institutions as the World Bank and the International Monetary Fund and, most of all, the capacity of governments to be interpreters of an economic policy, that is, to govern the movement of capital and commodities.

Social change

The most conspicuous and significant social innovation that came with the Golden Age was a reduction in the number of farmers. Until the mid-1950s, with the sole exception of Great

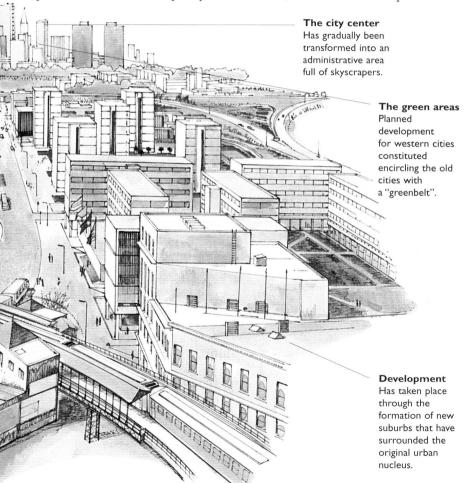

The city center
Has gradually been transformed into an administrative area full of skyscrapers.

The green areas
Planned development for western cities constituted encircling the old cities with a "greenbelt".

Development
Has taken place through the formation of new suburbs that have surrounded the original urban nucleus.

Britain, farmers had represented the highest percentage of the world's working population. The only important exceptions to this change were sub-Saharan Africa, Latin America, South and Southeast Asia, and China, where villages and fields still dominated the scene. We must not forget, however, that together these areas contained almost forty percent of the world's population. The drastic reduction in the number of farm workers and farmers and the increase in the world's production of foodstuffs were the consequences of a real agricultural revolution. In the West, the extremely rapid rise in agricultural production was caused by the massive use of capital and the widespread availability of farm machinery. In poorer areas of the world, this green revolution came about through the use of irrigation methods and the introduction of new high-yield strains of cereal grains.

One of the primary consequences of the reduction in the number of farmers was population growth in the cities, a trend that began in the Golden Age and continues to this day. The typical city of the most developed countries in Europe grew up around a historic center that was transformed into an administrative area that consisted of increasingly tall building that contained its expansion. These cities tended to disappear from the high rankings in the charts of the world's most heavily populated cities. Asian, Latin American, and African capitals, in contrast, developed and

THE WELFARE STATE
The welfare state became one of the causes of increased life expectancy in the West, partly as a result of health care systems and the increase in leisure time.

expanded often chaotically, with populations numbering many millions.

The Golden Age witnessed the expansion throughout the West of the principles and procedures that had been typical of Roosevelt's New Deal in the 1930s. The welfare state was the guarantor of its citizens' social security, health, and employment. The increase in the number of jobs that required more education was accompanied by the progressive expansion of the right to schooling, also guaranteed by the government. Social mobility became a fundamental characteristic of the Golden Age. The traditional working class, now with a social and political strength derived from the security of employment, continued to be one of society's most important components. The proliferation of international trade

The disabled
Their increased integration in society has been partially recognized.

World population In the course of the century this has increased dramatically, particularly due to the increase in life expectancy. While societies tend to get older in the West, in many countries, like Nigeria, the birth rate, and consequently the population turnover, is still very high.

did not induce governments to open their frontiers to international and intercontinental migrations of workers. However, internal migration and even migration of people from neighboring countries at times decisively influenced national economies. There were important changes, too, in the activities and role of women, both in the world of work and in public.

For roughly twenty years, between 1945 and 1965, the economy and society changed profoundly. Once again the change was ushered in by men and women who had lived through recent history, those who had experienced the Age of Catastrophe, along with the states, social classes, and national industrial concerns that existed before

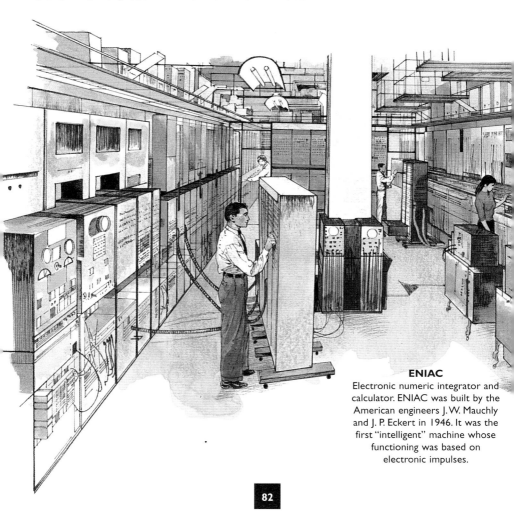

ENIAC
Electronic numeric integrator and calculator. ENIAC was built by the American engineers J. W. Mauchly and J. P. Eckert in 1946. It was the first "intelligent" machine whose functioning was based on electronic impulses.

the Golden Age. The change appeared to be oriented towards development, but it took place within political, economic, social, and cultural frameworks of the previous period. Only towards the end of the 1960s, with the coming of age of generations, social classes, and populations distant from or outside the Age of Catastrophe, did the world seem to enter a new era.

Technology

World War II had created a great demand for high-technology armaments. When the killing stopped, the impetus of big science continued to stimulate production in both the military and civilian industries.

The result was a technological explosion, with wide-ranging consequences in everyday life. New home

Medicine
In the 20th century there have been enormous advances; a noteworthy example is the discovery of penicillin by Alexander Fleming in 1928. Another important date is April 26, 1954, when mass vaccination against poliomyelitis began in the United States with the vaccine of Salk and Sabin.

A comparison
The first computer, ENIAC, occupied an area of about 1,500 square feet: quite different from the computers of today which can be put on a small desktop.

Yuri Gagarin

Soviet cosmonaut who made the first manned space flight on April 12, 1961 in his tiny capsule, Vostok. For the Soviets it was a great technological and prestigious success over the United States, which only one year later sent into orbit its own astronaut, John Glenn.

The moon

The most important date in the space race was July 21, 1969. On that day, after a journey of three days and more than 186,000 miles, Neil Armstrong and Edwin Aldrin set foot on the moon, while a third astronaut, Michael Collins, waited for them in orbit. The United States amazed the world, reaffirming their supremacy in space over the Soviet Union.

 appliances, like the refrigerator and the freezer were filled with foods manufactured using new methods—frozen foods, industrial-scale poultry farming, meats full of enzymes—or imported from distant places in fast airplanes. But the change went beyond food production. Virtually everything was transformed, from transport and communications to home furnishings and recreation.

Another great consequence of the new technological era was that scientific research became an essential aspect of economic growth. The success of a product was increasingly bound up with its popular appeal: the process of innovation became incessant and a growing proportion of production costs went into research. For their development and use in production, new technologies demanded large amounts of capital, considerable and continuous investments. This need for constant cash infusions also characterized the economic transformations that followed the Golden Age.

The Cold War

Much of the development in science and technology in the twentieth century was directly linked to the demands of the military-industrial complexes of the United States and the USSR, the two superpowers that had emerged victorious from World War II and dominated their respective areas of influence. The war had ended European domination of the international scene, and the United States was now the only country left to face down, in Europe and elsewhere, a communist country like the USSR. The latter had been strengthened by its industrial expansion, its victory in the war, and its acquisition of control over many Eastern European countries after the war when the Yalta conference divided the world into spheres of influence.

In the United States there was widespread apprehension about the communist threat and American programs of aid to European countries grew out of a determination to prevent crises and popular unrest and to strengthen the more moderate, pro-American parties.

Rivalry between the two superpowers was real and derived from their great strength. It was also a competition that stimulated the development of both contenders throughout the Golden Age. At the same time, this rivalry fueled the repression of internal dissent. In 1956 the USSR did not hesitate to use tanks against the Hungarian people in Budapest, and in the United States Senator Joseph McCarthy unleashed an investigation against many individuals with liberal and socialist ideas, accusing them of being communists or communist sympathizerss. The thermometer of the ideological climate—between the United States and Western Europe on one side and the USSR and Eastern Europe on the other—recorded high temperatures. This period was known as the "Cold War." Government officials

Nikita Khrushchev
Stalin's successor as leader of the Soviet Union. Khrushchev sought to shift military competition with the United States onto the economic plane.

The supply of arms
Supplying Third World armies with conventional weapons became normal policy for the leading countries of the two power blocs, which in this way succeeded in filling the world with armaments.

Suez

Two-thirds of the oil destined for Europe passed through the Suez Canal. When Egyptian president Nasser closed it in 1956 he sparked a conflict between Egypt and France, England and Israel, the result of which was to strengthen Arab nationalism.

RIVALRY BETWEEN THE SUPERPOWERS

Took place in the Third World. Each superpower sought to attract new states into its own sphere of influence, particularly through the supply of military aid.

GUINEA 1959

Czechoslovakian arms were supplied by Communist countries to the Guinea of President Sekou Touré.

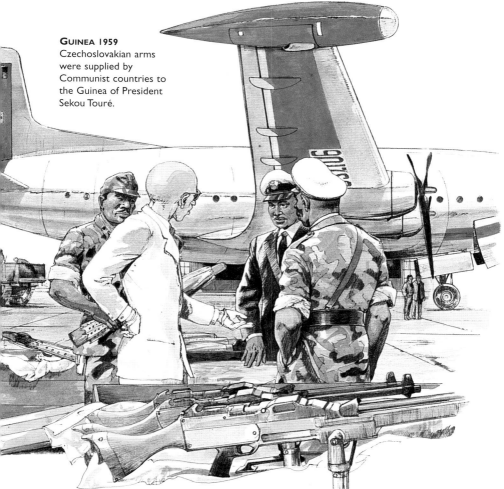

argued that each side had enough weapons to deter attacks by the other. Nevertheless, the threat of nuclear war was and is real.

The balance of terror

The superpowers' strategy was to establish a balance of terror based on their acquisition of nuclear armaments and sophisticated modern weapons. While the space race appeared to be more of a symbolic reflection of the competition, the real battlefield of the Cold War lay in regions distant from the United States and the USSR. Both sides sought to entice into their respective spheres of influence countries that had not yet formed an alliance with either power.

The governments of both blocs authorized their powerful military-industrial complexes to arm potential allies/clients—states, liberation movements, subversive groups—with conventional weapons. Both superpowers strained and paid a heavy price for this costly arms race: nuclear and strategic weapons for themselves, traditional weapons for all others.

Although the Cold War was founded on a balance of terror, moments of great tension and

THE BERLIN WALL
Erected on the night of August 12, 1961 by the communists of the East to block the migration of people to West Germany. The windows of the buildings of East Berlin overlooking it were walled up.

even actual conflicts did occur.

In 1950 North Korea, with the support of the USSR and China, invaded proAmerican South Korea. The United States interpreted the attack as an expression of Soviet communist expansion and sent troops to rebel the invaders. Military operations ended in 1953 after a conflict that cost 2.5 million lives and marked the first time that the United States was engaged directly with the Chinese army. After the Korean War, the conflict between the United States and USSR extended well beyond Europe to include the rest of the world, particularly Asia. In this new climate, the United States undertook extensive programs for the reconstruction of Japan and the relaunching of its economy. In Europe tension was particularly high in Germany, part of which belonged to the Soviet bloc. The city of Berlin was divided into the communist Democratic Republic and an area that was occupied by France, Great Britain, and the United States after the war. The wall built by the communists in 1961 to divide the city became the symbol of the world's division into two ideological and military blocs.

Countries that chose not to side with either bloc, the so-called non-aligned countries, experienced a period when they did not have the same costs as those aligned with a superpower.

In Asia

Several world political events in the postwar years marked the final and irreversible end of the international system that dominated before the war.

World War II, unlike its predecessor, had heavily involved European peoples and countries under colonial rule. With the end of war in 1945, the charter of the United Nations organization proclaimed the beginning of decolonization. Their participation in the conflict and the new world climate gave a definite boost to the national independence movements of colonized peoples. The cultural elite of the Indian subcontinent, for example, had been fighting for the independence for decades. This finally came in 1947, although deep divisions between Muslims and Hindus prevented the formation of a single state. Thus India and Pakistan were born following a dramatic migration of 17 million Hindus and Muslims, with many killings and atrocities by both factions.

In Asia, Burma, Malaya, the Philippines, and Indonesia won their independence. The People's Republic of

ONE PEOPLE, TWO RELIGIONS
The greatest obstacle to the formation of an Indian state was religious and political hostility between Muslims and Hindus.

EASTERN BENGAL
Proclaimed itself independent from Pakistan in 1971, thus creating the state of Bangladesh.

Indonesia

Proclaimed its independence in 1945 at the same time as the surrender of Japan. Ahmed Sukarno (in the photograph, with Mao Tse Tung) became president of the new state. After a conflict with the Dutch, who reclaimed their old colony, independence was finally recognized in 1948.

Two states

The population of the Indian subcontinent was divided into two states with a dramatic migration in opposite directions of more than 15 million people.

Incidents

During the mass migrations there were numerous incidents of hostility and bitter clashes resulting in approximately 500,000 deaths.

Kibbutzes
Colllective farms where the first Jewish immigrants were welcomed after their arrival in Palestine.

Soldiers
Nothing more than farmers who provided for the military defense of their own village.

The Arabs
Their villages lay a short distance from the kibbutzes of the Jews, who were regarded as invaders.

 China was born on October 1, 1949, after Mao Tse-Tung's communist army won first against the Japanese and then internal adversaries, the nationalists.

The drama of Palestine exploded in the Middle East. The world felt that it owed a profound debt to the Jews, victims of the Nazi genocide. More than half a million Jews had already emi-grated to Palestine, their historic home-land, in search of their own country. The Arab governments of the region, in support of more than one million Palestinians who also considered Palestine their home, opposed the formation of a Jewish state. The founding of the State of Israel in 1948 was the first act in the new history of the Jewish nation. At the same time, it marked the beginning

PALESTINE
In 1945, under British mandate,
it was populated by 1,250,000
Palestinians and 560,000 Jews
(many having immigrated between
the two wars, some residents
from Roman times).

The state of Israel In 1948, after the UN had proclaimed the partition of Palestine and the division of Jerusalem, Arab armies invaded the new state of Israel, which emerged victorious and gained land. Many Palestinians were forced to relocate to refugee camps in nearby Arab states.

of wars with the Arab states and constant military tension with the Palestinians.

The Algerian War
While Great Britain stepped down in Asia, principally through negotiations and diplomatic agreements, France initially had no intention of relinquishing its empire. In Indochina, their con-

flict with the Vietnamese allied with Ho Chi Minh led to a ruinous French defeat at Dien Bien Phu in 1954. Laos and Cambodia won independence, while Vietnam was divided at the seventeenth parallel between the communist North and the pro-American South.

In Africa, too, the French opposed the independence movement of the

THE BATTLE OF ALGIERS
Fought in 1957: it was a guerrilla
war of Algerian militants
supported and hidden by the
population. The tortures
perpetrated by the French army
provoked great indignation
in France.

Front de Libération National in Algeria. The conflict lasted from 1945 until 1962, the year of Algerian independence. During the Battle of Algiers in 1957, the world became aware of the strength of popular guerrilla warfare against a great and powerful army.

Once the country was independent, Algeria's prime minister Ben Bella set out to modernize it and, using income from the sale of oil, raise the standard of living of the Algerian people. However, he soon was confronted by Islamic fundamentalists and tribal groups. This anticipated the profound problems that would face a nation in search of its identity following a century of colonial rule.

The kasbah
The old Arab quarter of Algiers which represented the safest refuge for the guerrillas.

Indochina
Another theater of war for French colonialism had been Indochina.

Vietnamese troops under General Giap defeated the French at Dien Bien Phu in 1954.

The atrocities
Episodes of gratuitous violence against colonized peoples continued even in

the 1950s, as in the case of the bloody British repressions of the Mau Mau in Kenya, or in Malaysia.

The decolonization of Africa

Between 1957 and 1967 forty African states became independent from Belgium, France, and Great Britain. In decades of colonial rule, Europeans had generally failed to understand the specific ethnic, linguistic, and cultural identities of the various African peoples. As a result, the boundaries of the new states had been drawn up arbitrarily by the colonial powers. The Europeans handed political authority over to the nationalist elite whose parties had participated in political life during the years preceding independence. But authoritarian regimes often took power in these countries.

The new states, however, remained economically dependent, thus enabling their former rulers, together with the

Western Africa
In English-speaking Africa, for example in Nigeria, the struggle for independence was manifested from 1945 in the form of mass syndicalism. The Ghana of President Nkrumah appeared to be the model of emancipation because of its greater economic development.

THE CONGO
The assassination of president Patrice Lumumba in 1961 had the effect of demonstrating the difficulty of holding the country together.

Patrice Lumumba
Founder of the anti-colonialist movement of the Congo, whose unity he sought to guarantee against secessionist tendencies. His political adversary Tshombe was suspected of having ordered his assassination.

French Africa
The French favored the division of western and equatorial French-speaking Africa. The Guinea of Sekou Touré emerged, as did Cameroon, the scene of a bitter struggle for national independence.

The UN
Sent its own troops into the Congo though their presence there was ineffective.

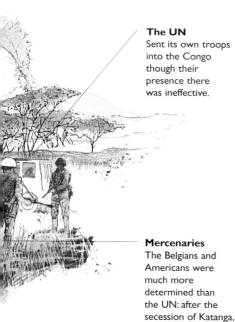

Mercenaries
The Belgians and Americans were much more determined than the UN: after the secession of Katanga, with the help of France they had Mobutu installed in power, who began a regime of corruption and inefficiency.

two superpowers, to continue their political involvement (also called neo-colonialism). A tribal revolt was often only a simple cover for the intrusion of a foreign power, as in the case of the assassination of the anti-colonial leader Patrice Lumumba in the Congo in 1961.

Even today there remains a widespread tendency to consider Africa and its problems as a single, undifferentiated entity. Nothing could be further from the truth. The differences are visible in the profound differences generated by particular experiences of colonial rule and struggles for independence. These various experiences have led to different economic interests and therefore such specific problems as environmental degradation and famine. Knowing this is vital to understanding the many Africas south of the Sahara—Western, Eastern and Central Africa, Portuguese Africa, and the Horn of Africa—that differ according to their own experience of decolonization.

Revolutions

The politics of Latin America and the world were shaken in 1959 by the victorious Cuban revolution led by Fidel Castro, one of whose chief lieutenants was the Argentinian doctor Ernesto "Che" Guevara.

The Cuban revolution caused great tension between the United States and the USSR. The country was the only left-wing regime in Latin America and so sided with Third World revolutionary movements. Che particularly became a popular symbol

THE CULTURAL REVOLUTION
August 18, 1966, in Peking, witnessed the outbreak of the Cultural Revolution of the Red Guards, a group composed of millions of young people.

Intellectuals
The object of violent and bitter persecutions, they were dragged in procession through the streets with a list of their errors.

Mao Tse Tung
He accused the leaders of the Communist Party of having taken the path of capitalism and invited the people to fire on their headquarters.

The little red book
A summary of the writings of President Mao, a text of pure propaganda which, as such, achieved its objectives. It became a cult object even in the West.

毛澤东思
PROPAGANDA TEAM OF MA

The Red Guards
The level of violence they reached was such that Mao himself, in 1969, called for the army to intervene in order to prevent further degeneration.

among young social activists throughout the world.

Following a rise to power at the head of an anti-imperialist movement, with formidable support from the peasant population, Mao and the Chinese Communist Party plunged into a utopian venture known as the "Great Leap Forward." The aim was to transform a political victory into great economic boom, encouraging the peasants, who lacked adequate machinery, to strive towards exceptional production levels. This policy proved catastrophic and led to famines that from 1958 to 1962 caused the death of thirty million people. The Chinese Cultural Revolution led by Mao was an even stronger influence on young Europeans during the 1960s. Despite being contested even within his own party, Mao, a shrewd politician, regained his authority in China by unleashing the Cultural Revolution of 1966. Initially a student movement supported by the

The future is China
In the 1980s the Chinese economy grew from 8 to 10 percent a year. Between 1984 and 1996 the gross national product doubled. The country has changed its face but the political regime is still very severe.

military, it later erupted into acts of violence that devastated China. The Cultural Revolution ended in 1976 with Mao's death, and China embarked on a period of reform promoted by Deng Xiaoping.

Vietnam

More than by the misbegotten Chinese Cultural Revolution, the world's ideological climate in the second half of the 1960s was dominated by the Vietnam War.

At the start of the decade, the pro-American government of South Vietnam clashed with partisan forces supported by the communist government of North Vietnam. American presidents, from John F. Kennedy on, saw Vietnam as a bulwark in the

GUERRILLA WARFARE
It proved superior against the most powerful army in the world, that of the United States. Its strengths lay in the combat techniques as well as in the extraordinary determination of a people struggling for its own freedom.

THE JUNGLE
The environment most favored by the Vietcong for ambushing American patrols.

Reporters
Every day they followed the progress of operations with their cameras and notebooks.

defense of Western values in Southeast Asia. From 1965 the United States bombed North Vietnam and stepped up its military presence in the South. The war's cost, in terms of human lives and financial resources, aroused bitter opposition in the United States. South Vietnam was no match for the North's National Liberation Front and following the withdrawal of American troops in 1973, North Vietnam won the final victory on April 30, 1975. With the Vietnam War, the international role and prestige of the world's greatest superpower reached its all-time low since the beginning of the Golden Age.

1968: a watershed

The Golden Age witnessed an increase in the student population as well as an

Cambodia
On 17 April 1975 the Khmer Rouge (photo), communist guerrillas, seized power in the Cambodian capital Phnom Penh.

Laos
A communist group of the independence movement in Laos, Pathet Lao, seized power in the country in December 1975.

Helicopters
Permitted the rapid evacuation of wounded or surrounded soldiers.

Hiding places
These were underground and enabled the guerrillas to wait patiently and choose the most propitious moment for attacking the enemy.

Bob Dylan
Symbol of folk music, he took part in the march in the name of a generation that aspired to a better society.

THE GREAT MARCH
300,000 people marched through Washington on August 28, 1964. It was the most memorable undertaking of the struggle led by Martin Luther King, Jr. for the civil rights of African-Americans.

MARTIN LUTHER KING, JR.
Black minister and leader of the struggles of African-Americans for civil rights, he was assassinated on April 4, 1968 in Memphis, Tennessee.

The protest
On the podium of the final of the 200 meters at the Olympic Games in Mexico City in 1968, Tommie "Jet" Smith and John Carlos, who had arrived first and third respectively, raised their black-gloved fists to protest against racial discrimination.

May in France
In May 1968 students in Paris created a permanent mobilization with processions, general assemblies, and committee meetings.

 extraordinary rise in literacy rates. Students became the protagonists of the celebrated revolts of 1968. The young would-be revolutionaries demanded a better society, and criticism of authority was widespread. The year has been compared to others in nineteenth century Europe, such as 1830 or 1848, years of great revolutionary upheaval. No revolution took place in 1968: despite their passion and numbers, the students were unable to carry out sweeping change on their own. They were, however, a catalyst for other groups and were responsible for a profound change in social behavior.

Student revolts in America started in 1960: students mobilized in protest against the racial segregation of African-Americans.

The second great theme of protest among young Americans was against the "dirty war" in Vietnam. At the University of California at Berkeley, Harvard, and Yale, as at all the most prestigious American universities, students burned their draft cards publicly. In Japan too, the Vietnam War was the main reason for student protest. From May 1968, Europe became the epicenter of the student movement. The themes common to the movement in other countries—Vietnam and criticism of consumer society—were accompanied in Berlin and West Germany by strong opposition to German laws governing public order. For the first time since the World War II, a law enabled Germany to take action without Allied authorization. Germans

The invasion of Prague
Soviet tanks interrupted the process of the democratization of Czechoslovakian political life. The country was invaded and the party leaders dismissed.

DRUGS
The use of drugs became widespread among the young people of the Woodstock generation.

FIVE HUNDRED THOUSAND
This was the number of the people who attended the three-day festival of music in the name of peace and free love, almost as if taking part in a dress rehearsal for a different society.

also protested against a revival of Neo-Nazi activities. The revolutionary movement was strong in Italy and particularly so in France: in Paris there were days of great intensity in May. In both these countries, students broke their isolation from other parts of society. Their protests took on political forms associated with the social struggles of traditional labor unions intent on showing the strength of the workers. In Spain and Mexico, students, and indeed many elements within their societies united against the regimes in power.

SEXUAL FREEDOM
Introduced as a new social value in the late 1960s.

In the closed monolithic bloc of the East European countries, dominated by the USSR, 1968 was also a year of great protest, especially in Czechoslovakia. There protest assumed the form of a liberalization of political and intellectual life, both in society and the Communist Party. Criticism of socialist regimes and Soviet domination spread to other countries such as East Germany, Hungary, and Poland. The Soviet Union decided to put a halt to the "Prague Spring" and on August 21, 1968 sent tanks from countries of the Soviet bloc into Czechoslovakia with 250,000 armed soldiers against the nonviolent protest of the students and people of Prague.

The entry on the political stage of a generation that had not experienced the Age of Catastrophe, a generation whose sense of security was quite different from that of previous generations, brought with it changes in culture and lifestyle that were far more deep-rooted than is generally recognized.

CALIFORNIA ROCK
Expressed the conviction that music could really change the world.

THE DECADES OF CRISIS: 1973–1999

The economy became increasingly transnational: the keyword now is globalization. States and traditional institutions seemed to weaken, unemployment rose and, in international politics, the old order was replaced by a new order.

In the early 1970s the course of the twentieth century again changed direction as the Golden Age gave way to the Decades of Crisis. Just what happened? During the decades of world development, the economy had progressed within a world order: the leading country in the West was the United States, which was opposed to the Soviet Union, the leader of the Eastern bloc. During the Golden Age, the countries of Europe and Japan gradually increased their economic power and competed with the United States in increasingly intense world trade.

The globalization of the economy
Several important events occurred between 1971 and 1973. The dollar—the main currency of the world economy—was no longer convertible to gold,

THE WEAPON OF PETROLEUM
In October 1973, during the Jewish festival of Yom Kippur, Egypt and Syria attacked Israel, which, with massive American support, successfully counter-attacked. The oil-producing Arab countries blocked supplies to the West.

OPEC
On December 22, 1973, in Teheran, the Organization of Petroleum Exporting Countries decided on a 130 percent increase in the price of crude oil. The organization was comprised of Venezuela (1); Kuwait (2); Saudi Arabia (3); Iraq (4); Iran (5); Ecuador (6); Qatar (7); Indonesia (8); Arab Emirates (9); Libya (10); Gabon (11); Nigeria (12); Algeria (13).

1   2   3   4

The oil crisis
In the West it was deeply felt. The reaction was to limit energy consumption drastically.

A second crisis
This took place in 1979–1980 following the revolution in Iran. The price of a barrel of crude oil increased two and a half times.

5 6

7

8

9

10

11

12   13

which meant that it could be devalued. The oil-producing countries suspended the sale of crude oil to Western countries and then raised the price. An economy that had grown internationally under the control of states was now replaced by a transnational economy that had escaped those controls.

Until this time the history of the twentieth century was a history of growing interrelation between economies, a phenomenon evident in all the main periods of the century. In the final decades, however, it is no longer appropriate to speak of economies that interact. They have been overtaken by a unified transnational economy that reduces the capacity of states to control. During the Golden Age, nations played a crucial role in development by means of programs, regulation, direct intervention in leading sectors, and welfare policies. In this phase of globalization of the economy, the function and importance of states became increasingly inadequate. The result was that the economy of the world market had no government capable of managing and dealing with its crises.

In concrete terms, globalization occurred as a consequence of continual changes in the international division of labor. Countries that had once imported industrial products now produced them, due to their lower labor costs. At the same time, large manufacturing concerns tended to sell their products on the entire world market.

EUROPE

Since the 1950s Europe has been on the path towards unification. European unity is one of the most efficient political answers to the globalization of the economy. Western Europe has its own currency and its own economic policy and citizens of the European Union move freely from country to country.

The fall of centuries-old frontiers

From 1998 people can move freely between most European countries. For those who travel between Berlin, Rome, London, Paris... there is no longer any passport control.

A multi-ethnic society
Passport control is in force only for those people who do not come from the European Union.

Western societies are becoming increasingly multi-ethnic due to the arrival of people emigrating from poorer countries.

The globalization of the economy and the difficulty of administering it rationally were the context for the crisis that began to affect the economy in the 1970s.

Where there was once full employment, unemployment began to rise. Prosperity was supplanted by poverty. Social inequalities became increasingly pronounced within single states and among rich states and poor states. Governments were no longer capable of regulating the behavior of markets that extended beyond national confines. At the same time, they were crushed beneath the weight of expenditure for systems of public insurance, social security, and pensions. With the appearance of an economic recession, public spending increased, while the crisis itself reduced revenues. We should not consider the crisis as a fall in production or trade (which in fact did not happen). Rather, it was a result of difficulties in governing the economy and, especially, as a phenomenon of rising unemployment.

The first half of the twentieth century and the Golden Age had seen the progressive reduction in the number of agricultural workers, who were replaced by the growing practice of mechanized farming techniques; industry, however, had absorbed those laborers. Automation and the technological revolution now eliminated labor from industry and services faster than the market economy could create new employment. The creation of supernational institutions, such as the European Union, was one of the

possible answers to the crisis, at least as far as Western Europe was concerned. Every region of the world, however, had to face problems and find specific answers that were not at all easy to come by.

International order

For forty-five years, from the end of World War II until 1990, the world was divided into three parts. The First World—Western countries in the United States sphere of influence— and the Second World—Eastern countries under Soviet domination— remained virtually stable. Up to a certain time, they experienced continuously increasing production and prosperity. The Third World, including most of Asia, Africa, and Latin America, was a nonaligned universe whose individual components oscillated between the two superpowers, a vast, fragile, and politically unstable area where revolutions were frequent and unpredictable.

It has been calculated that from 1945 until halfway through the 1980s, almost twenty million people were killed in more than one hundred wars and conflicts that for the most part took place in the Third World. Both the United States and the Soviet Union had often encouraged and supported armed uprisings in the Third World. The United States had fought the danger of an expansion of its adversary's influence by means of economic aid, ideological propaganda, and support of regional wars and in some cases military insurrection.

The stadium of Santiago in Chile
Sadly famous because after Pinochet's takeover of power it was transformed into a terrible detention center for political dissidents and unwanted foreigners.

General Pinochet
On September 11, 1973 he led a bloody coup d'état against Allende, who was murdered.
In 1998 Pinochet was put on trial in Europe for his crimes against humanity.

Apartheid
A policy of racial segregation practiced by the white elite of South Africa against the black majority, ever since the state's independence (1910). In 1994, with the end of apartheid, the black leader Nelson Mandela was elected president of South Africa.

During the 1960s and 1970s, Latin America fell victim to antidemocratic military coups in many states, including Brazil, Bolivia, Argentina, and Uruguay. In Chile, in 1973, a military coup strongly backed by the United States put an end to the left-wing, democratically elected government of Salvador Allende. The torture, murder, kidnapping, and exile of political adversaries were the atrocious but routine practices of these military regimes.

Africa, Asia, and Central America were the scene of several political revolutions during the 1970s. The last European Fascist regime, in Portugal ended in 1974. As a result, Angola, Mozambique, and Guinea Bissau, for a long time engaged in a struggle for freedom from Lisbon, finally won their independence. Other uprisings for independence took place in Madagascar, Congo, and the Rhodesias. A widespread mass movement got underway in South Africa against the rule and apartheid politics practiced by the white minority: with the electoral victory of Nelson Mandela in 1994, a black man became the first president of

THE GOVERNMENT OF UNIDAD POPULAR
The government of Salvador Allende had a program of modernization and nationalization of public services, banks and, in particular, the country's precious copper mines.

The invasion of Afghanistan
Between 1979 and 1989 the USSR waged an illfated war against the mujaheddin (Islamic fighters for the faith) in support of the communist government.

Cambodia
In the 1970s the regime of Pol Pot and his Khmer Rouge, in the name of egalitarian fanaticism, exterminated a quarter of the country's population.

the new democratic and multiracial state.

In Southeast Asia, following the United States' withdrawal of troops from Vietnam, Laos and Cambodia became communist countries. In Cambodia, the regime of Pol Pot's Khmer Rouge added yet another genocide to an already long list of slaughter in the twentieth century.

In 1979 the Nicaraguan Revolution broke out in Central America. The revolutions of the 1970s accompanied and stimulated a new period of confrontation in the Cold War between the United States and the Soviet Union: the two superpowers clashed indirectly through their respective allies in the world's hot spots. In Afghanistan, the Soviet army intervened directly for the first time since the last world conflict outside the area of influence assigned to the Soviet Union at Yalta. The twelve-year occupation of the central Asian

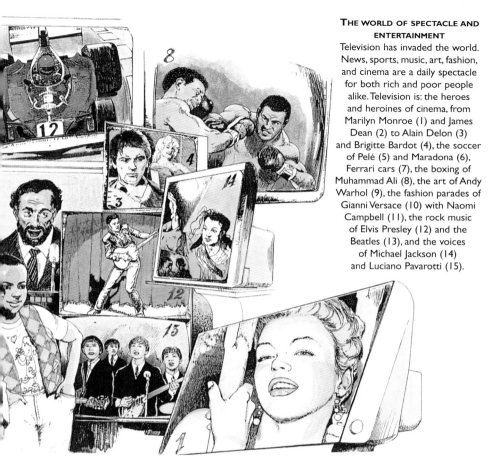

Television has invaded the world. News, sports, music, art, fashion, and cinema are a daily spectacle for both rich and poor people alike. Television is: the heroes and heroines of cinema, from Marilyn Monroe (1) and James Dean (2) to Alain Delon (3) and Brigitte Bardot (4), the soccer of Pelé (5) and Maradona (6), Ferrari cars (7), the boxing of Muhammad Ali (8), the art of Andy Warhol (9), the fashion parades of Gianni Versace (10) with Naomi Campbell (11), the rock music of Elvis Presley (12) and the Beatles (13), and the voices of Michael Jackson (14) and Luciano Pavarotti (15).

country proved to be a serious military and economic strain on the USSR, and the conflict ended in much the same way as Vietnam had for the Americans.

The metropolitan areas of First World countries, particularly in Western Europe, were struck by the phenomenon of international terrorism. Political, ethnic, or religious groups, Italian left-wing extremists, Irish or Basque independence groups, Palestinians and Islamic extremists all engaged in armed insurrection and spectacular terrorist actions that aimed to exploit the potential of mass communication, as happened during the 1972 Olympic Games in Munich.

But revolutionary movements during these years were not traditional in character. They were not identified with revolutionary minorities that were seen as the vanguards of change; rather they allied themselves with vast movements of urban masses.

One example of this took place in 1979, in Teheran, the capital of Iran, a city whose population had grown from one to six million inhabitants in fifteen years. Here the people, guided by the Shi'ite Islamic clergy, overthrew the modernist regime of the Shah and founded an Islamic Republic. This event marked the spread of Islamic fundamentalist movements that, employing terrorism, called for a "holy war" against Israel, the West, and moderate Arab countries. The world's major war, however, which started in 1980 and lasted eight years, was fought between Iran and Iraq, whose leader, Saddam Hussein, attempted an expansionist policy in the name of pan-Arab unity and came into conflict with the Iranian Muslim clergy.

The fall of communism

The fall of communist regimes in such countries as the German Democratic Republic, Hungary, Poland, Czechoslovakia, and Romania also came about at the end of the 1980s, as a result of virtually bloodless uprisings of urban masses. The initial phases of dissent against the Romanian dictator Ceausescu by the crowds of Bucharest were even filmed by live television and broadcast to homes all over the world. The crisis that led the communist world dominated by the Soviet Union to die out had roots in the economic stagnation of that great country, aggravated, in the 1970s, by competition with the United States, and by uncontrolled military spending. However, the Soviets did export oil and were not hurt

The Olympic athletes continued to train, living in the Olympic village in a climate of great tension.

PALESTINIAN TERRORISM
In the 1970s it was an increasingly international phenomenon. Airplane hijackings, bombs, spectacular actions often performed under the eyes of television cameras, aimed to strike at Europe and the United States for their so-called imperialist policies.

The Olympic Games in Munich
In 1972 Palestinian terrorists of the Black September organization massacred eleven Israeli athletes in the Olympic Village.

In Europe
European terrorism was often linked to the struggles of ethnic and religious minorities. This was the case, for example, with ETA of the Basque countries, or the IRA, for the reunification of Northern Ireland with the rest of the island. Political terrorism developed after the protests of the 1960s: in Italy with the Red Brigades.

The Ayatollah Khomeini
Exiled for many years, Khomeini was an enemy of the Western-style modernization undertaken by the shah Reza Pahlavi. In 1979 he replaced him as the leader of Iran.

FUNDAMENTALISM
Movements and groups of various religions which reject modernism and fanatically defend what they consider to be fundamental religious principles. In the 1960s, some Catholics protested against the renewal promoted by the 2nd Vatican Council wanted by Pope John XXIII. In the 1970s, in the Islamic world, fundamentalism became an important factor in world politics.

The great Satan
The name the Islamic revolution used to describe the United States. On November 4, 1979 Islamic extremists captured 53 hostages at the American embassy in Teheran and held them hostage for 444 days.

by the rise in the cost of petroleum introduced by OPEC countries in 1973.

The young communist leader, Mikhail Gorbachev—elected secretary of the Soviet Communist Party in 1985 — unexpectedly and in the space of just a few years reached an agreement with the United States for the progressive destruction of missile arsenals (Washington summit, December 1987), an initiative that led to the end of the Cold War. At the same time, he renounced Soviet domination over Eastern European countries, abandoning the various communist parties to their own fates and enabling general uprisings against the various regimes. The most dramatic conclusion to all this came with the fall of the Berlin Wall (1989) and the consequent reunification of Germany into a single state.

In the second half of the 1980s, the USSR moved rapidly towards the

Peace between Egypt and Israel
Under the mediation of the United States, it was signed in September 1978 between the Egyptian president Sadat and the Israeli premier Begin. Islamic extremists later assassinated the Egyptian leader.

Bombs with submunitions

The end of Communism

Led to the constitution of new independent national states.
From the dissolution of the Soviet Union came: the Baltic republics of Estonia, Latvia, and Lithuania; the central European states of Russia, Belarus, Moldova, and the Ukraine; the Caucasian states of Armenia, Azerbaijan, and Georgia; and the five republics of central Asia, Kazakstan, Kyrgyzstan, Tajikstan, Turkmenistan, and Uzbekistan. From Yugoslavia, Slovenia, Macedonia and, at the price of a bloody conflict, Serbia, Croatia and Bosnia Herzegovina. Czechoslovakia was split between the Czech Republic and Slovakia. Germany, instead, returned to being united in 1992 after the collapse of the Democratic Republic and the fall of the Berlin Wall.

Reagan and Gorbachev
The two presidents who, as well as characterizing an era in their own countries, met several times.

"Smart bombs"
Were so called because they were capable of striking a precise objective with the aid of sophisticated technology.

precipice. Gorbachev pushed for a democratic and pluralist political system. But the debate on economic reforms saw the disintegration of the political and social authority that had traditionally made the economy work, resulting in crisis and the collapse of living standards and social balances. The new autonomy and strength of the Russian Federal Republic accelerated the break-up of the great multiethnic and supernational state—first a tsarist empire, then a communist state—which then split into fifteen states.

Without a world order

The world's sovereign states numbered 49 in 1919, 66 in 1976, and 122 in 1964. Today there are 182 countries represented at the United Nations. However, the increase in the number of nations

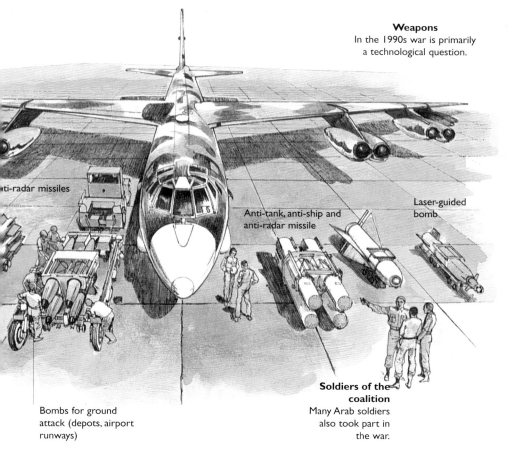

Weapons
In the 1990s war is primarily a technological question.

ti-radar missiles

Laser-guided bomb

Anti-tank, anti-ship and anti-radar missile

Soldiers of the coalition
Many Arab soldiers also took part in the war.

Bombs for ground attack (depots, airport runways)

has been accompanied by a growing impotence on the part of the governments to control the economy and by an increasingly marked absence of order in the international system.

Immediately after the fall of the USSR and the end of communism everywhere but China, Cuba, and Albania, to respond to the attack of Saddam Hussein's Iraq on Kuwait (August 2, 1990), the only remaining world superpower, the United States, organized a coalition of states under the aegis of the United Nations.

On January 17, 1991 the world watched the live television broadcast of the bombing of Baghdad: the most frequent comment was that world order was conducting a normal police operation against a criminal regime. For a while there was the feeling that the old bipolar order had been replaced by a new order under the leadership of the United States. In reality, however, the bloody ethnic struggles in the new states emerging from the break-up of Yugoslavia and the genocide caused by weapons or famine have revealed the absence of any real balance. Having now outgrown the order of the Three Worlds, the planet appears divided simply into rich areas and poor areas. The citizens of strong, stable areas like the European Union, the United States, and Japan might mistakenly feel themselves immune to the instability and bloodbaths occurring either near or far away. In reality, the crisis of traditional state institutions and the lack of control over the world economy jeopardize the condition of the entire planet.

The world's population has reached six billion. With a present growth rate of about one billion per decade, we must already urgently pose the question: just how many people can live on the Earth?

SARAJEVO

The city that stands as a symbol of the century: the scene of the event that sparked World War I, a conflict between peoples that ended an era. Until the end of 1995 the capital of Bosnia was bombarded every day by the Bosnian Serbs. The conflict caused 200,000 deaths and created 3 million refugees.

Hunger and war
A tragic scourge affecting Africa in particular, where ethnic conflicts lead to the creation of millions of refugees, as in the case of Rwanda in 1994.

Armenia
Ethnic conflicts also involve the territories of the former Soviet Union: Christian Armenia and Muslim Azerbaijan bitterly fought each other in 1993–1994.

Internet
The great information network that links the world by the year 2000 reaches only a portion of the world's population.

The ethnic war
Respects no one. Bullets can fly at any time, even during a funeral.

Index